CW00541373

F1errari

Feierabend

F1er

Rainer W. Schlegelmilch

rari

Hartmut Lehbrink

Foreword by Jean Todt

INH
CONT

Vorwort von Jean Todt

Schon als Junge hatte ich diese Passion für Autos und den Motorsport. Natürlich war Ferrari in meiner Wertschätzung ganz oben angesiedelt. Mit 26 kaufte ich meinen ersten, für achthundert Dollar, einen 250 GT California Spider. Es kostete mich allerdings 3000 Dollar, ihn zu restaurieren, und so veräußerte ich ihn wieder und erwarb von dem Erlös mein erstes Appartement.

Schon immer hatte der Name Ferrari eine besondere Aura und etwas Magisches. Warum das so ist, weiß ich nicht. Als ich Peugeot Motorsport leitete, entschloss ich mich, ein Buch über die Marke mit dem Löwen zu schreiben. Als Verfasser des Vorworts kam nur einer in Frage: Enzo Ferrari. Zum Glück erfüllte sich mein Wunsch. 1985 fand ich mich in Maranello ein zu einem Treffen mit dem Commendatore. Wir aßen zu Mittag in seinem Büro in Fiorano, zusammen mit seinem Sohn Piero, Franco Gozzi und Marco Piccinini. Selbst in meinen kühnsten Träumen wäre es mir nicht in den Sinn gekommen, dass ich einmal Chef der Scuderia sein würde.

Erste Kontakte zu Präsident Montezemolo gab es 1992. Bernie Ecclestone hatte mich informiert, dass Luca meinen Anruf erwartete. Im August jenes Jahres trafen wir uns in Bologna. Weitere Zusammenkünfte folgten, bis wir uns einig waren. Am 1. Juli 1993 übernahm ich die Leitung der Gestione Sportiva. Wir waren beide ganz schön kühn, der Präsident, weil er mir eine derartige Chance gab, ich selbst, weil der Zeitpunkt dafür nicht gerade günstig war. Es handelte sich um die größte Herausforderung, die ich mir vorstellen konnte, und es gab sogar Leute, die mir dringend davon abrieten. Alain Prost zum Beispiel gab mir zu verstehen, ich würde Ferrari niemals in den Griff bekommen. Er musste es schließlich wissen, da er zwei Jahre lang in Maranello eine Schlüsselrolle gespielt hatte. Zwischen 1994 und 1999 dachte ich häufig, dass er und die anderen Recht hatten.

Am Ende schufen wir ein ungemein starkes Team – mit der nie endenden Unterstützung durch Montezemolo. Stets widerstand er dem Druck, der auf ihm lastete, sich noch einmal neu zu orientieren. Stets glaubte er an den Weg, den wir eingeschlagen hatten. Dies führte zu unserem Dream Team, mit Michael Schumacher als Pilot, der wahrscheinlich nicht nur der größte Fahrer aller Zeiten ist, sondern auch ein guter Freund. 1999 gewannen wir den Konstrukteurstitel und dann dreimal hintereinander beide Meisterschaften. Michael überbot Fangios Rekord von fünf Championaten ein und Ferrari holte sich fünf hintereinander. Das gab es noch nie.

Seit dem Tag, an dem ich die Aufgabe bei Ferrari übernahm, hat die Scuderia in über fünfzig Grand Prix gesiegt. Manchmal liefen die Dinge auch schief, aber das hat uns nur noch mehr zusammengeschweißt. Unser Stil zu arbeiten hat sich nie geändert: mit beiden Beinen fest auf dem Boden, sogar jetzt, wo alles optimal läuft. Die schwierigen Zeiten haben wir dabei keieswegs vergessen, die Jahre, in denen wir den Titel beim Finale verloren und Michaels Unfall in Silverstone. Er hat dem Team dafür nie die Schuld gegeben. Wir wollen weiter siegen. Wenn ich eines Tages gehe, war ich beteiligt an einem Drittel aller Ferrari-Siege und einem wichtigen Kapitel in der Geschichte eines Rennstalls, der eine Legende ist und es immer sein wird.

Oktober 2002

Foreword by Jean Todt

Ever since I was a small boy I had a passion for cars and for motor sport. Naturally, Ferrari was uppermost in my mind. When I was twenty-six, I acquired my first Ferrari, paying eight hundred dollars for a 250 California Spider. Shortly afterwards, having spent three thousand dollars restoring it, I was able to buy my first apartment with the proceeds from selling it.

The Ferrari name always had a special aura and something magical about it, although I cannot explain why. I recall that when I was running Peugeot Motorsport, I decided to write a book about the Lion marqueís successes with the 205. There was only one person I wanted to write the foreword, Enzo Ferrari. Luckily my wish came true. It was in 1985 that I found myself in Maranello to meet the Commendatore. We lunched together in the Fiorano office, along with his son Piero, Franco Gozzi and Marco Piccinini. Never in my wildest dreams could I imagine that, one day, I would be in charge of the Scuderia!

My first contact with President Montezemolo dates back to 1992. Bernie Ecclestone told me that Montezemolo was expecting my call and in August of that year, we met for the first time, in Bologna. There were further meetings until we reached an agreement and, on 1st July 1993, I took control of the Gestione Sportiva. We had both been pretty brave: the president for having offered me such an opportunity and I for having accepted at a time that was far from easy. It was the biggest challenge I could have dreamed of, even if many people told me I should not have taken it on. For example, Alain Prost confided in me that I would never turn Ferrari around. If he told me that, having spent around two years at Maranello, then there was cause for concern. From 1994 to 1999, I often thought that Prost and the others had been right.

In the end, we managed to create a very strong team, thanks to the never ending support of President Montezemolo, who never gave in to the pressure which urged him to change. He always believed in the path we had chosen. This led to our success and a dream team with a driver like Michael Schumacher, who is not only possibly the greatest driver of all time, but also a good friend. In 1999, we took the Constructors' title, followed by a trio of both championships. Michael has managed to surpass Fangio's all-time record of title wins and Ferrari has won five consecutive championships, something it had never done before.

Since the day I took on this task with Ferrari, the Scuderia has won over fifty Grands Prix. When things were going badly, we still remained united and that made us stronger. We continue to work in the same way, keeping our feet firmly on the ground, even now when everything is going well. We have not forgotten the difficult times - the years in which we lost the title at the final round and Michael's accident at Silverstone, for which he has never blamed the team. We want to continue winning. When I leave, I will be able to say I played a part in a third of Ferrariís victories and have contributed to writing an important chapter in the story of a team which is and will always be a motoring legend.

Oktober 2002

Vorwort von Rainer W. Schlegelmilch

Ein Buch über Ferrari zu gestalten, noch dazu mit meinen eigenen Aufnahmen der letzten 40 Jahre, ist ein aufregender Blick in die Vergangenheit und zugleich eine Zeitreise durch mein Leben. Der Firmengründer Enzo Ferrari, den ich jeweils nur einmal im Jahr beim Grand Prix in Monza erlebte, beeindruckte mich durch sein Charisma und sein »italienisches« Temperament. Auch die Fahrer, die von ihm auserwählt waren, wurden durch das Wappen mit dem springenden Pferd am Fahrzeug zu Halbgöttern.

Ferrari war der Rennstall, dessen Piloten ich am meisten fotografierte, angefangen mit Phil Hill, Ricardo Rodriguez und Lorenzo Bandini. Eindrucksvolle Porträts machte ich von John Surtees und Jacky Ickx, zu dem sich auch eine persönliche Freundschaft entwickelte. Damals standen die Rennwagen noch vor den Boxen im Freien und alles, auch die Männer am Lenkrad, war jederzeit für mich und meine Kamera erreichbar. Es folgten Niki Lauda, Jody Scheckter und einer, der nie Weltmeister war, aber durch die Verbindung mit dem cavallino rampante zum Giganten aufstieg: Gilles Villeneuve. Sie alle ließen mich Bilddokumente schaffen, deren Dramatik und Ausdrucksstärke heute nur noch gelegentlich möglich ist.

Nach 20 mageren Jahren führten Michael Schumacher, Rubens Barrichello, Luca di Montezemolo und Jean Todt mit seinem Team die Scuderia zu einer gewaltigen Wiederauferstehung. Ich bin glücklich, dass ich durch meine Fotografie einen Beitrag zur Dokumentation dieses Erfolgs leisten darf.

Rainer Schlegelmilch

Foreword by Rainer W. Schlegelmilch

To create a book on Ferrari, and with my own pictures from the last 40 years at that, permits an exciting look back in the rear-view mirror as well as time travel through my own life. Founding father Enzo, who I saw only once a year at Monza, impressed me by his almost palpable charisma and his Latin temperament. The drivers he elected became objects of my awe and reverence through the Prancing Stallion on their cars.

Ferrari was soon the racing stable whose protagonists became my favourite objects, beginning with Phil Hill, Ricardo Rodriguez and Lorenzo Bandini. With early portraits I was able to convey the greatness of John Surtees and Jacky Ickx, who was to become a good friend of mine. In those years the cars stood in the open in front of the pits so everything, including the men who drove them, was within my and my camera's reach. Then came Niki Lauda, Jody Scheckter and one of my heroes who would never be world champion: Gilles Villeneuve. Through his association with the cavallino rampante he became a giant all the same. They all in their respective context gave me the opportunity to produce pictorial documents, whose drama and expressiveness have become rare today.

After twenty lean years Michael Schumacher, Rubens Barrichello, Luca di Montezemolo and Jean Todt with his team have led the Scuderia along the path to a most impressive renaissance. I thoroughly enjoy being able, through my photos, to contribute my mite to the documentation of this success.

D ie Herausforderung liegt im Wandel. Zwar steht seit ihren offiziellen Anfängen 1950 auf der Sache Formel 1 drauf. Aber es ist ständig etwas anderes drin. Schon in der ersten Dekade ändert die Rennlegislative die Rahmenbedingungen zweimal einschneidend. Ursprünglich haben die Hersteller die Qual der Wahl zwischen 1,5-Liter-Maschinen mit Kompressor oder 4,5-Liter-Triebwerken ohne. 1952 folgt eine für höchste Würden umgewidmete Formel 2, maximaler Hubraum zwei Liter. 1954 stocken die Herren der Rechte in Paris auf 2,5 Liter auf. Gewiss lässt die Scuderia Ferrari ein paar Federn, vor allem während des triumphalen Mercedes-Intermezzos 1954 und '55 und angesichts des Umbruchs ausgangs des Jahrzehnts. Charles und John Cooper haben die Heckmotor-Revolution angezettelt und in Jack Brabhams beide Titel 1959 und '60 umgemünzt. Aber man mauert auch bereits am eigenen Mythos, mal überzeugend, mal mit massiver Hilfe des Ministeriums der Glücksgöttin Fortuna, Dezernat Piloten und Pisten. Den ersten Sieg für die Ferrari-Variante des italienischen Rennrots vermerken die Chronisten für den 14. Juli 1951 in Silverstone durch den fülligen Argentinier Froilan Gonzalez, den sie den Pampasstier nennen. 1952 und '53 wächst kein Kraut gegen den Mailänder Doppel-Champion Alberto Ascari, der elf von 15 Rennen gewinnt. Juan Manuel Fangios Meisterschaft 1956 ist ein nobles Präsent seines Teamgefährten Peter Collins, der ihm zweimal in entscheidenden Augenblicken den eigenen Wagen überlässt. Und auch Mike Hawthorn siegt 1958 nur knapp – mit einem Punkt Vorsprung vor seinem glücklosen Landsmann Stirling Moss im Vanwall.

Challenge arises from change. From the very beginning in 1950, the label on the product has been Formula 1. But the contents have continually changed. Within the first ten years, motor racing's governing body massively altered the rules twice. Originally, the manufacturers had the choice between blown 1.5 litre engines or normally aspirated 4.5 litre units. In 1952 what was basically Formula 2 followed, boldly elevated into the highest realms of the business because the giants were gone. In 1954 the Paris-based rule masters opted for 2.5 litre power-plants. The Scuderia Ferrari certainly lost a few feathers, particularly during the triumphant Mercedes return in 1954 and '55 and the upheaval towards the dying years of the decade. It was then that Charles and John Cooper triggered the rear-engine revolution, notching up two titles with Jack Brabham at the wheel in 1959 and '60. But Ferrari's own myth was already in the making, sometimes convincing, sometimes due to massive assistance from Lady Luck. The first victory for the Ferrari variant of Italian racing red was recorded on 14 July 1951, with chubby Argentinian Froilan Gonzalez in charge, a.k.a. the Pampas Bull. In 1952 and '53 the Milan double champion Alberto Ascari was untouchable, winning eleven out of a total of 15 races. Juan Manuel Fangio's 1956 crown was a noble present, courtesy of his team mate Peter Collins, who let him have his own car twice when it really counted. And Mike Hawthorn's championship victory in 1958 turned out to be a close one, too, with his luckless compatriot Stirling Moss in a Vanwall breathing down his neck, just one little point behind.

Monaco 1950, Alberto Ascari

Monza (I) 1951

Spa-Francorshamps (B) 1951, Alberto Ascari and Luigi Villoresi

Silverstone (GB) 1951, José Froilan Gonzalez, 1st winner for Ferrari

Nürburgring (D) 1952, Ascari leading

Monza (I) 1952, Ascari leading Farina

1952

Rouen (F) 1952, 1st row for Alberto Ascari, Giuseppe Farina and Piero Taruffi

Silverstone (GB) 1953, start, Alberto Ascari leading José Froilan Gonzalez and Juan Manuel Fangio

Nürburgring (D) 1953, Alberto Ascari

Bern (CH) 1953, Alberto Ascari, winner

Monza (I) 1954, Alberto Ascari leading Juan Manuel Fangio

Reims (F) 1954, José Froilan Gonzalez

Monaco 1955, Maurice Trintignant, winner

Monaco 1955, Eugenio Castellotti

Buenos Aires (RA) 1955, José Froilan Gonzalez

Reims (F) 1956, Juan Manuel Fangio

Monza (I) 1956, Luigi Musso leading Eugenio Castellotti and Juan Manuel Fangio

Rouen (F) 1957, Mike Hawthorn

Rouen (F) 1957, Luigi Musso

Aintree (GB) 1957, Peter Collins

Monza (I) 1957, Wolfgang Graf Berghe von Trips

Reims (F) 1958. Mike Hawthorn and Luigi Musso

1958

Monaco 1959, Jean Behra

1959 Phil Hill

1959

Avus (D) 1959, Tony Brooks, winner, leading Phil Hill, Dan Gurney

Buenos Aires (RA) 1960, Wolfgang Graf Berghe von Trips

Monaco 1960, Phil Hill

Die Saison 1961 - ein Ruhmesblatt in Rot. Erst spät hat Enzo Ferrari die Provokation durch die Engländer wie Cooper und Lotus angenommen. Ihre Piloten sitzen schon längst in kleinen und leichten Rennwagen, und zwar vor den Motoren. Das erste Jahr der Anderthalb- literformel aber haben sie verschlafen. Und so trumpft der störrische Alte von Maranello groß auf, mit dem Typ 156/F1. Dessen Fahrwerk lässt zwar zu wünschen übrig. Aber sein V6 ist mit 180 und später 190 PS um mindestens 25 Pferdestärken potenter als die Climax-Vierzylinder der Konkurrenz von der Insel. Gleichwohl wird 1961 auch zum schwarzen Jahr für die Scuderia. In die Entscheidung, welcher Ferrari-Pilot Champion wird, mischt sich der Renntod ein. In Monza stirbt Graf Berghe von Trips. Der Sieg des Amerikaners Phil Hill aber hinterlässt keine Spuren: Die glorreichen 156/F1 werden später zerschreddert.

The 1961 season – a page of glory in red. Only late had Enzo Ferrari taken up the gauntlet thrown at his feet by the British such as Cooper and Lotus. For some time their drivers had already sat in small and light racing cars and had done so in front of the engine. But they had slept through the first season of the new 1.5 litre formula. And so the stubborn Maranello sex- agenarian swept the board with his shark-nosed 156/F1. It did not handle too well. But its V6 engine with its 180 and later 190 bhp was at least 25 bhp more potent than its Climax four- cylinder competitors from the Island. But 1961 was also a tragic year for the Scuderia. The needle match between its drivers about who was to be world champion was decided by Death when Count von Trips was killed at Monza. No trace was left of amiable American Phil Hill's victory as later the glorious 156/F1 cars were all scrapped.

World Championship

1 Phil Hill (34)
1 Wolfgang von Trips (33)
3 Stirling Moss (21)
3 Dan Gurney (21)
5 Richie Ginther (16)
6 Innes Ireland (12)
7 Jim Clark (11)
7 Bruce McLaren (11)
9 Giancarlo Baghetti (9)
10 Toni Brooks (6)
11 Jack Brabham (4)
11 John Surtees (4)
13 Olivier Gendebien (3)
13 Jack Lewis (3)
13 Graham Hill (3)
13 Jo Bonnier (3)
17 Roy Salvadori (2)

Aintree (GB) 1961, Wolfgang Graf Berghe von Trips, winner

Monza (I) 1961, Ferrari

Nürburgring (D) 1961, Phil Hill

Auf das fette Ferrari-Vorjahr folgen 1962 Flaute und Frust. Das deutet sich schon an, als nach dem Ende der Saison 1961 Schlüsselpersonal wie Technikchef Carlo Chiti und Rennleiter Romolo Tavoni kündigt, um in dem keimenden und rasch wieder verkümmernden ATS-Rennstall des venezianischen Grafen Volpi neues Heil zu suchen. Chitis nervöser Kronprinz Mauro Forghieri und Tavonis ewig Ränke schmiedender Nachfolger Eugenio Dragoni müssen sich erst einarbeiten. Das Projekt 156/F1, eben noch unschlagbar, stagniert und verkommt am Ende. Die englische Konkurrenz hingegen gebietet über glänzende Fahrwerke und die voll ausgereiften Achtzylinder von Coventry-Climax und BRM. Die Meisterschaft gerät zum Duell zwischen Graham Hill (BRM) und Jim Clark (Lotus). Die Scuderia muss sich mit einem Sieg auf einem Nebenschauplatz begnügen: durch den wilden Belgier Willy Mairesse beim Großen Preis von Brüssel – in einem Gebrauchtwagen Baujahr 1961.

After the strong breeze swelling the Ferrari sails in the year before, the team rolled in the doldrums in 1962. That had been signalled when key personnel like technical director Carlo Chiti and race manager Romolo Tavoni walked out in disgust after the 1961 season to join the disastrous ATS venture of the Venetian Count Volpi. Chiti's nervous heir apparent Mauro Forghieri and Tavoni's successor, the ever scheming Eugenio Dragoni, needed time to adjust. The 156/F1 project, once almost invincible, stagnated and eventually went to waste. Ferrari's English competitors, however, sported excellent chassis and fully developed eight cylinder engines from Coventry-Climax and BRM. The fight for the title became a duel between Graham Hill (BRM) and Jim Clark (Lotus). The Scuderia, however, had to be content with victory in a non-championship event, scored by the wild Belgian Willy Mairesse at Brussels – in the 1961 model.

World Championship

1 Graham Hill (42)
2 Jim Clark (30)
3 Bruce McLaren (27)
4 John Surtees (19)
5 Dan Gurney (15)
6 Phil Hill (14)
7 Tony Maggs (13)
8 Richie Ginther (10)
9 Jack Brabham (9)
10 Trevor Taylor (6)
11 Giancarlo Baghetti (5)
12 Lorenzo Bandini (4)
12 Ricardo Rodriguez (4)
14 Willy Mairesse (3)
14 Jo Bonnier (3)
16 Innes Ireland (2)
16 Carel Godin de Beaufort (2)
18 Masten Gregory (1)
18 Neville Lederle (1)

1962

Nach einer Kollision mit Taylors Lotus verbrennt der Ferrari von Willy Mairesse in Spa am Straßenrand.

After a collision with Taylor's Lotus Willy Mairesse's Ferrari was reduced to ashes in Spa.

Spa-Francorchamps (B), Phil Hill

Spa-Francorchamps (B), Willy Mairesse

Spa-Francorchamps (B), Ricardo Rodriguez and Phil Hill

Nach dem Dahintrödeln im Leerlauf im Jahr zuvor legt man bei Ferrari wieder den ersten Gang ein. Neuzugang John Surtees erweist sich, wie erwartet, als Gewinn. Als siebenfacher Motorradchampion hat der eigenwillige Brite unter dem Grafen Domenico Agusta gedient, einem Renn-Aristokraten ähnlich seinem neuen Boss. Seine Qualitäten: ein brillanter Ingenieur, ein besessener Versuchsfahrer, ein begnadeter Pilot – jemand, der nie die Flinte ins Korn wirft. Mit dem Commendatore eint ihn die Wahlverwandtschaft der Eigenbrötler, mit Mauro Forghieri die Hingabe an die Sache. Erste Dividende stellt sich ein mit seinem Sieg beim Großen Preis von Deutschland in der Ausbaustufe B des bisherigen Tipo 156. Der 156 Aero einen Monat später in Monza später zollt bereits dem Geist der neuen Zeit seinen Tribut: Halbmonocoque wie im Flugwesen, innen liegende Dämpfer und Federn vorn, Bremsen am Differential hinten, Sitzposition wie im Liegestuhl.

After idling along the year before, Ferrari engaged first gear, as it were, to cope with the 1963 season. Newcomer John Surtees proved the asset everybody had expected him to be. The stubborn Briton had won seven motorcycle world championships for the Count Domenico Agusta, who was of the same aristocratic and autocratic mould as his new boss. His qualities: a superb engineer, an indefatigable test driver, a brilliant talent at the wheel – somebody who never gave up. Because of their affinity as marked individuals, he at once forged a strong bond with the Commendatore and found a congenial partner in young Mauro Forghieri. To prove his point, Surtees won the German Grand Prix in the "B" version of the Tipo 156. The 156 Aero, which appeared at Monza a month later, was already a state-of-the-art racing car – with its semi-monocoque as used in aircraft building, front inboard springs and dampers, rear brakes located on the differential, and a deck chair-like seating position.

World Championship

1 Jim Clark (54)
2 Graham Hill (29)
2 Richie Ginther (29)
4 John Surtees (22)
5 Dan Gurney (19)
6 Bruce McLaren (17)
7 Jack Brabham (14)
8 Tony Maggs (9)
9 Innes Ireland (6)
9 Lorenzo Bandini (6)
9 Jo Bonnier (6)
12 Gerhard Mitter (3)
12 Jim Hall (3)
14 Carlo Godin de Beaufort (2)
15 Trevor Taylor (1)
15 Ludovico Scarfiotti (1)
15 Jo Siffert (1)

Monaco, John Surtees

1963

Im zweiten Jahr seiner Verweildauer bei Ferrari greift der Surtees-Faktor. Big John wird Welt-meister – wenn auch knapp. Die beiden Grands Prix von Deutschland und Italien hat er gewonnen. Aber erst in den letzten Minuten des Finallaufs in Mexico City kommt es zur Nagel-probe. Die anderen Titel-Prätendenten Jim Clark im Lotus und Graham Hill eliminieren sich selbst beziehungsweise werden ausgeschaltet, da Surtees' Teamkollege Lorenzo Bandini den BRM des schnauzbärtigen Briten brutal von der Piste boxt. Der 158/F1 ist einer der schönsten Ferrari-Rennwagen, die je gebaut wurden, und auch der besten. Zu seinem exzellenten Fahr-werk gesellt sich wie bei der englischen Konkurrenz ein Achtzylinder. Bereits im August 1963 fertig gestellt, musste sich der V8 mit der mächtigen Stimme in zahlreichen Tests erst an die Ernährung durch eine Einspritzanlage gewöhnen. Als Dank macht Enzo Ferrari seinem Star-piloten seinen Dienstwagen zum Geschenk.

In the second year of his Ferrari service the Surtees factor bore fruit. Big John became world champion – by a hair's breadth, having just won the German and the Italian Grands Prix. He took the title by a single point in a three-way decider in Mexico City, with Jim Clark in a Lotus and Graham Hill snapping at his heels. But the two other pretenders dropped out or were elimi-nated, as Surtees' team mate Lorenzo Bandini brutally pushed the moustached Briton's BRM from the track. The Tipo 158/F1 was one of the most beautiful Ferrari Formula 1 cars ever and one of the best. Its excellent semi-monocoque chassis was mated to an eight cylinder engine like its English competitors'. That V8 unit with its raucous voice was ready as early as August 1963. But in an endless series of tests it had to be reconciled with being fed by injection rather than carburettors. In a generous gesture, Enzo Ferrari later presented his star driver with his championship vehicle.

World Championship

Monaco, Lorenzo Bandini

Zandvoort (NL), John Surtees

Im letzten Jahr der alten Formel regiert die Koalition aus dem Vollgas-Genius Jim Clark und dem genialisch konzipierten Lotus 33 uneingeschränkt. Für die Scuderia ragen als Bestwerte aus einem Meer von Mittelmaß die beiden zweiten Plätze in East London (Südafrika) und Monaco heraus, brüderlich geteilt von der Fahrer-Riege John Surtees und Lorenzo Bandini. Der 512/F1, mit Ferraris erstem V12 im Extremwinkel von 180 Grad, müsste eigentlich 1512 heißen wegen seines Hubraums von 1,5 Litern und den Zylindern im Dutzend. Konstruktive Macken suchen ihn heim, seine direkte Bosch-Einspritzung muss ihre guten Gaben auf winzige Verbrennungs-einheiten von 124 ccm verteilen, der Sektor Reifen gereicht zum Ärgernis. Noch eine Premiere: Die rote Hülle besteht aus Kunstharz und Glasfaser. Teamleader John Surtees begegnet dem Neuen mit Misstrauen und steigt erst in Silverstone vom Vorjahresmodell um – zu spät.

In the last year of the old formula, the coalition of the ultimate racing driver Jim Clark and the congenitally conceived Lotus 33 reigned supreme. The Scuderia, however, was reduced to mediocrity. The two second places in East London and Monaco, shared between its drivers John Surtees and Lorenzo Bandini, were its best results of the season. The correct designation of its 512/F1 car, propelled by Ferrari's first V12 engine with the extreme bank angle of 180 degrees, ought to have been 1512 because of its capacity of 1.5 litres and the number of its cylinders. It was plagued by mechanical gremlins, its direct Bosch fuel injection had to cope with unit displacement of only 124 cc. and tyre complications aggravated certain performance difficulties. Another first: Its body was the first to be built by Ferrari completely of glass-packed resin. Team leader John Surtees did not love the 512. Only at Silverstone did he change over to it from the preceding year's car – too late.

World Championship

1 Jim Clark (54)
2 Graham Hill (40)
3 Jackie Stewart (33)
4 Dan Gurney (25)
5 **John Surtees (17)**
6 **Lorenzo Bandini (13)**
7 Richie Ginther (11)
8 Mike Spence (10)
8 Bruce McLaren (10)
10 Jack Brabham (9)
11 Denny Hulme (5)
11 Jo Siffert (5)
13 Jochen Rindt (4)
14 Pedro Rodriguez (2)
14 Ronnie Bucknum (2)
14 Richard Attwood (2)

Monaco, Lorenzo Bandini leading John Surtees

Monaco, Lorenzo Bandini

1965

Zandvoort (NL), Lorenzo Bandini

Zandvoort (NL), John Surtees

Zandvoort (NL), Lorenzo Bandini

Die Saison 1966 läutet eine zwanzigjährige Ära von Dreilitern ein. Ferrari ist im Grunde gut gerüstet. Man verfügt über einen gestandenen V12 mit einem Gabelwinkel von 60 Grad aus den Sportwagen der Marke, anfänglich mit 325 PS etwas schwächlich auf der Brust, ab Monza mit Dreiventilköpfen und 380 PS hinreichend stark. Unterdessen versucht das Lager der Opposition ziemlich orientierungslos Tritt zu fassen. Aber wieder wird die Scuderia von Reifenproblemen gelähmt. In Zandvoort testet man Pneus von Goodyear und feuert den bisherigen Lieferanten Dunlop in Monza zugunsten von Firestone. Überdies stellt sich Stunk im Zwischenmenschlichen ein: John Surtees bekommt sich in die Wolle mit Rennleiter Dragoni und dem anderen Briten im Team, dem Versuchsingenieur und Piloten Mike Parkes. Dokumentiert durch den John-Frankenheimer-Film Grand Prix erringt Big John in Spa bei pladderndem Ardennen-Regen seinen größten Sieg – und geht, mitten in der Saison.

The 1966 season ushered in a twenty-year era of three-litre cars. Ferrari should have had the edge as it had at its disposal a proven V12 60 degree sports car engine. At the beginning, its output stood at a somewhat meagre 325 bhp. From Monza onwards, three valves per cylinder provided it with an impressive 380 bhp. Meanwhile, the opposition were struggling to come to terms with the new regulations. But again the Scuderia was crippled by tyre problems. At Monza, the former supplier Dunlop was abandoned in favour of Firestone. Apart from that, human relations were strained. There was lots of needle between John Surtees and Machiavellian team manager Dragoni, as well as his compatriot Mike Parkes, who was a test engineer as well as being a race driver also in the Scuderia's services. Well documented by John Frankenheimer's film epic Grand Prix, Big John scored his greatest win at Spa, unfazed by torrential rain – and called it a day, in the middle of the season.

World Championship

1 Jack Brabham (42)
2 John Surtees (28)
3 Jochen Rindt (22)
4 Denny Hulme (18)
5 Graham Hill (17)
6 Jim Clark (16)
7 Jackie Stewart (14)
8 Mike Parkes (12)
8 Lorenzo Bandini (12)
10 Ludovico Scarfiotti (9)
11 Richie Ginther (5)
12 Mike Spence (4)
12 Dan Gurney (4)
14 Bob Bondurant (3)
14 Jo Siffert (3)
14 Bruce McLaren (3)
17 John Taylor (1)
17 Bob Anderson (1)
17 Peter Arundell (1)
17 Jo Bonnier (1)

Monaco, Lorenzo Bandini

Spa-Francorchamps, John Surtees, winner

1966

Nürburgring (D), 11 Scarfiotti, 9 Bandini, 10 Parkes

Nürburgring (D), Mike Parkes

1966

Monza (I), Ludovico Scarfiotti, winner

Wie 1965 bleibt auch die Saison 1967 für Ferrari sieg- und damit frucht- und freudlos. Schlimmer noch – als die neue Nummer 1 im Team ist Lorenzo Bandini nie in die großen Fußstapfen hineingewachsen, die John Surtees bei seiner vorzeitigen Kündigung im Jahr zuvor hinterlassen hat. Die Erwartungen einer ganzen Nation lasten auf ihm und das wird ihm in Monaco zum Verhängnis: Fahrfehler an der Schikane, flammendes Inferno, fatale Verbrennungen. Die Stafette wird aufgenommen von Chris Amon, der im Fürstentum sein erstes Rennen für die Scuderia bestritten hat. Der Neuseeländer wird nie einen Grand Prix gewinnen, hat aber ein gutes Händchen mit Rennwagen und treibt die Entwicklung voran. Mit dem 312/F1 findet er ein Objekt mit viel Potential vor, ab Monza mit Vierventilköpfen und 410 PS und einem Wohlklang, den man einfach gehört haben muss.

196

Like 1965, the 1967 season remained without victory and, as a consequence, fruit- and joyless for the Scuderia. Worse still: Lorenzo Bandini as the team's new number one was never able to follow in the big footsteps left behind by John Surtees after his premature demise the year before. Instead, he was weighed down by the expectations of a whole nation. That burden turned out to be a lethal one at Monaco: mistake at the harbour chicane, fiery inferno, fatal burns. The challenge was taken up by Chris Amon, who had driven his first race for the Scuderia in the Principality. Never was the New Zealander to win a race. But he definitely knew how to handle a racing car and was an outstanding test driver. The Tipo 312/F1 was an object full of potential, from Monza onwards with four valves per cylinder and a melodiousness worth hearing emanating from its complicated exhaust system.

World Championship

1 Denny Hulme (51)
2 Jack Brabham (46)
3 Jim Clark (41)
4 John Surtees (20)
4 Chris Amon (20)
6 Pedro Rodriguez (15)
6 Graham Hill (15)
8 Dan Gurney (13)
9 Jackie Stewart (10)
10 Mike Spence (9)
11 John Love (6)
11 Jochen Rindt (6)
11 Jo Siffert (6)
14 Bruce McLaren (3)
14 Jo Bonnier (3)
16 Bob Anderson (2)
16 Mike Parkes (2)
16 Chris Irwin (2)
19 Ludovico Scarfiotti (1)
19 Guy Ligier (1)
19 Jacky Ickx (1)

Monaco, Chris Amon

Monaco, Lorenzo Bandini

Monaco, Lorenzo Bandini

Beim zweiten Lauf der Saison in Jarama startet Chris Amon aus der Pole-Position und führt 42 Runden lang. Das wirkt wie ein günstiges Omen. Doch dann bleibt es beim Sieg des Ferrari-Novizen Jacky Ickx in Rouen, bei Schmuddelwetter und auf maßgeschneiderten Regenreifen. Das ist eine dürftige Ausbeute für den 312/F1 jenes Jahres. Denn die entscheidenden Faktoren ergänzen einander harmonisch: ein umgängliches und gut liegendes Chassis, ein kraftvoller V12 mit einem günstigen Drehmomentverlauf, die dazu passenden Firestone-Pneus. In Spa erhebt sich ein zierlicher Heckflügel über den vorderen Ausläufern des Triebwerks, austariert durch breite Spoiler beidseits der Nase. Die Evolution schreitet zügig voran. In Monza, einem beliebten Forum für Ferrari-Innovation vor den heimischen tifosi, lässt sich das hintere Leitwerk sogar schon vom Piloten hydraulisch verstellen. Diesmal staunt sogar der sonst auf die Sensation abonnierte Mr. Lotus Colin Chapman.

19

In the second race of the season at Jarama Chris Amon started from pole position and led for 42 laps. That seemed to be a good omen. But then there was just one victory, notched up by Ferrari novice Jacky Ickx at Rouen, on a semi-wet track and using made-to-measure rain tyres, a poor yield for that year's version of the 312/F1. All decisive factors complemented each other harmoniously: a well-balanced and driveable chassis, a powerful V12 unit with an excellent torque curve, the functional tyre characteristics of the Firestones. At Spa, the first wing in Formula 1 was mounted not far from the driver's head, the aerodynamic load it engendered being countered by wide front spoilers on either side of the nose. And evolution marched on rapidly. At Monza, a favourite stage for Ferrari innovation in front of the tifosi, the angle of the rear wing was controlled hydraulically by the driver. Even Mr. Lotus, Colin Chapman himself, the most inventive brain of them all, was baffled.

World Championship

Rouen (F), Jacky Ickx, winner

Rouen (F), Jacky Ickx, winner

1968

Nürburgring (D), Chris Amon

Nürburgring (D), pole for Jacky Ickx, 2nd Chris Amon

Nürburgring (D), Jacky Ickx

Monza (I), Jacky Ickx

Monza (I), Jacky Ickx

Monza (I), Jacky Ickx

Monza (I), winner Denny Hulme, Jacky Ickx 3rd

usgangs der Sechziger gehen Ferrari endgültig die lebenswichtigen Lire-Milliarden aus.
Am 18. Juni 1969 pilgert der Commendatore ins Fiat-Hauptquartier Turin. Aus der Audienz bei Konzernboss Gianni Agnelli gehen beide mit erhobenen Häuptern hervor. Die große Mutter Fiat nimmt die Nobelschmiede in Maranello mit 50 Prozent ihrer Anteile unter ihre Rockschöße und garantiert ihr Überleben. Enzo bleibt Chef und darf ungestört in seinem Rosengärtlein walten, der Rennabteilung. Auf den Pisten geht es den roten Rennern unterdessen dreckig. In Silverstone wirft Chris Amon das Handtuch, der bislang die Alleinvertetung der Marke innegehabt hat. Auch der Mexikaner Pedro Rodriguez kann das Ruder nicht herumwerfen. Am Wochenende des Großen Preises von Deutschland legt man gar eine schöpferische Pause ein: Der Tipo 312 ist übergewichtig und leidet an Macken des Fahrwerks sowie des auf 436 PS erstarkten, aber wenig flexiblen V12.

In the late sixties, Ferrari definitely ran out of the billions of lire necessary for the Prancing Stallion to survive. On 18 June 1969 the Commendatore journeyed to the Fiat headquarters in Turin. He shook hands on a contract with Gianni Agnelli which resulted in two winners. Fiat took 50 percent of the Ferrari stock, which would guarantee the survival of the noble Maranello manufactory. Enzo remained President and was allowed to do as he pleased as head of the racing department. Meanwhile, his cars were having a bad time. In Silverstone, Chris Amon, who had been the sole representative of the marque so far, threw in the towel. In the second half of the season, it was Mexican Pedro Rodriguez who was unable to wrench the wheel round. At the German Grand Prix, the red racers even stayed at home. The 1969 Tipo 312 was too heavy and plagued by excessive weight and problems regarding its chassis and V12 engine, which reached 436 bhp but was not flexible enough.

World Championship

1 Jackie Stewart (63)
2 Jacky Ickx (37)
3 Bruce McLaren (26)
4 Jochen Rindt (22)
5 Jean-Pierre Beltoise (21)
6 Denny Hulme (20)
7 Graham Hill (19)
8 Piers Courage (16)
9 Jo Siffert (15)
10 Jack Brabham (14)
11 John Surtees (6)
12 Chris Amon (4)
13 Richard Attwood (3)
13 Vic Elford (3)
13 Pedro Rodriguez (3)
16 Johnny Servoz-Gavin (1)
16 Silvio Moser (1)
16 Jackie Oliver (1)

Monaco, Chris Amon

Monaco, Chris Amon

Monaco, Chris Amon

Monaco, Chris Amon

Monaco, Chris Amon

Zandvoort (NL), Chris Amon

Clermont-Ferrand (F) Chris Amon

Der Fortschritt besteht im Rückgriff. Das Heil, befindet Ferrari-Technikchef Mauro Forghieri, liege in einem breiten Triebwerk mit niedrigem Schwerpunkt. Das gab's schon mal: im 512 von 1965 und im Zweiliter-Bergspider von 1969. In beiden Fällen lagen die Zylinderbänke einander horizontal gegenüber. Daher die Bezeichnung 312/B (für Boxer) für den Neuen. Frühe Tests während der Saison 1969 erweisen sich als viel versprechend, obwohl Chris Amon dem Projekt vor seiner Fahnenflucht eine vernichtende Expertise ausstellt. Auch mit den Fahrern tut man einen guten Griff. Nach einem Jahr bei Brabham ist Jacky Ickx zurückgekehrt. Und der Tessiner Clay Regazzoni gehört zu den Entdeckungen des Jahres 1970 wie der Brasilianer Emerson Fittipaldi und der Franzose Francois Cevert in anderer Leute Diensten. Mit dem Sieg des Belgiers auf dem neuen Kurs von Zeltweg kehrt man in den Kreis der Gewinner zurück. Drei weitere folgen. Alles, so scheint es, wird gut.

19

Sometimes the essence of progress is a step back. So technical chief Mauro Forghieri decided a low, wide engine would have advantages over the existing V12. There were recent precedents, in the 512 Formula 1 model of 1965 as well as in the two-litre Spider contesting the 1969 European hillclimbing championship. In both cases the cylinder banks were horizontally opposed. That is why the new car was called 312/B (for Boxer). Early testing in 1969 was promising although Chris Amon slammed the concept. Ferrari's driver choice was fortunate to boot. Jacky Ickx had returned after a year with Brabham. And Ticinese Clay Regazzoni was one of the revelations of the 1970 season, like Brazilian Emerson Fittipaldi and Frenchman Francois Cevert, who served other masters. The Belgian ace's victory on the new Zeltweg track spelt the Scuderia's return into the winner's circle. Three more followed. All was well, it seemed.

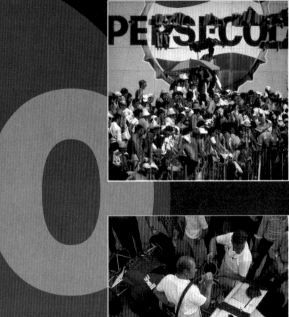

World Championship

1. Jochen Rindt (45)
2. **Jacky Ickx (40)**
3. **Clay Regazzoni (33)**
4. Denny Hulme (27)
5. Jack Brabham (25)
5. Jackie Stewart (25)
7. Pedro Rodriguez (23)
7. Chris Amon (23)
9. Jean-Pierre Beltoise (16)
10. Emerson Fittipaldi (12)
11. Rolf Stommelen (10)
12. Henri Pescarolo (8)
13. Graham Hill (7)
14. Bruce McLaren (6)
15. Mario Andretti (4)
15. Reine Wisell (4)
17. **Ignazio Giunti (3)**
17. John Surtees (3)
19. John Miles (2)
19. Johnny Servoz-Gavin (2)
19. Jackie Oliver (2)
22. Dan Gurney (1)
22. François Cevert (1)
22. Peter Gethin (1)
22. Derek Bell (1)

Monaco, Jacky Ickx

Hockenheim (D), pole for Jacky Ickx

Hockenheim (D), Jacky Ickx leading

Hockenheim 2.8.1970

Hockenheim (D), Jacky Ickx 2nd, winner Jochen Rindt

Zeltweg (A), Clay Regazzoni leading

Zeltweg (A), Jacky Ickx

Zeltweg (A), Jacky Ickx, winner

Monza (I). Clay Regazzoni

Monza (I), Jacky Ickx, pole

Monza (I), Clay Regazzoni, Jacky Ickx

Monza (I), Clay Regazzoni, winner

Monza (I), Clay Regazzoni

Jarama (E), Jacky Ickx

Jarama (E), Jacky Ickx' car after crash, Mauro Forghieri

In der Startrunde von Jarama trifft. Olivers BRM den Ferrari von Ickx mitschiffs. Beide Wagen gehen in Flammen auf.

On the opening lap in Jarama, Oliver's BRM hit Ickx' Ferrari amidships. Both cars were engulfed in flames.

Vor dem Hintergrund der abgelaufenen Saison wirkt das Grand-Prix Jahr 1971 wie ein gebrochenes Versprechen. Gewiss beschert Mario Andretti der Scuderia zum Einstand einen schönen Sieg in Kyalami. Und in Zandvoort zündet Jacky Ickx eines seiner Feuerwerke auf nasser Strecke. Das Konzept hinter dem 312/B ist gut. Am Detail muss indessen gefeilt werden. Mit mehr Bohrung und weniger Hub bringt es sein Boxer-Triebwerk auf eine höhere Leistung bei gestiegenen Drehzahlen (470 PS bei 12 600/min, vorher 450 PS bei 12 000/min). Viel Zuwendung wird der Aufhängung zuteil: Wegen seiner breiten Niederquerschnittsreifen beutelt der 312/B2 seine Insassen mit Vibrationen. Eine Zeitlang sind die Feder-/Dämpfer-einheiten hinten fast horizontal über Getriebe und Differential angesiedelt – ohne Erfolg. Ab Holland sieht man sich wieder auf die konventionelle Lösung zurückgeworfen. Manchmal, wie in Watkins Glen, wird sogar der Vorjahreswagen wieder aus der Garage geholt.

19

Seen against the backdrop of the season before, the 1971 grand prix year came like a broken promise. Certainly new Ferrari recruit Mario Andretti ran out a clear winner of the Kyalami season opener. And at Zandvoort, Jacky Ickx displayed his accustomed wet weather fireworks. The concept behind the 312/B was good. But it required numerous detail changes. With enlarged bore and shorter stroke, higher revs and an increased output were reached (470 bhp at 12,600 rpm, 1970: 450 bhp at 12,000 rpm). Much work was dedicated to the suspension. The 312/B2's drivers were shaken by vibrations because of its wide low-profile tyres. For some time, its spring/damper units were mounted almost horizontally above its gearbox and differential. That unusual arrangement did not pay. Starting with Holland, Forghieri and his men opted for the conventional layout again. Sometimes, like in Watkins Glen, it was even necessary to dust off the old model.

World Championship

1 Jackie Stewart (62)
2 Ronnie Peterson (33)
3 François Cévert (26)
4 Jacky Ickx (19)
5 Jo Siffert (19)
6 Emerson Fittipaldi (16)
7 Clay Regazzoni (13)
8 Mario Andretti (12)
9 Peter Gethin (9)
9 Pedro Rodriguez (9)
9 Chris Amon (9)
9 Denny Hulme (9)
9 Reine Wisell (9)
14 Tim Schenken (5)
15 Howden Ganley (5)
16 Mark Donohue (4)
17 Henri Pescarolo (4)
18 Mike Hailwood (3)
19 John Surtees (3)
19 Rolf Stommelen (3)
21 Graham Hill (2)
22 Jean-Pierre Beltoise (1)

Montjuich (E), Clay Regazzoni

1971

Montjuich (E), Jacky Ickx

Zandvoort (NL), Clay Regazzoni

Silverstone (GB), Jacky Ickx, Emerson Fittipaldi, Ronnie Peterson

Silverstone (GB), Clay Regazzoni leading Jacky Ickx

Silverstone (GB), Jacky Ickx

Silverstone (GB), Jacky Ickx

Nürburgring (D), Jacky Ickx

Monza (I), start

Monza (I), Jacky Ickx

Dem Ergebnis des Großen Preises von Deutschland 1972 haftet ein Hauch von Déjà-vu an. Jacky Ickx siegt vor Clay Regazzoni, beide Ferrari – wie in Zeltweg 1970. Das ist's auch bereits in jener Saison und es bedarf schon der konzertierten Aktion zweier Ausnahme- piloten auf dem Nürburgring, der damals noch zu Recht als die schönste und schwierigste Rennstrecke der Welt bezeichnet wird. Ansonsten werden für das ungleiche Gespann Besuche auf dem Podium rar, nach zwei zweiten Plätzen in Jarama und Monaco sowie einem dritten in Buenos Aires für Ickx sowie einem dritten Rang für Regazzoni in Spanien. Noch immer bereitet der 312/B2 Kopfzerbrechen. Bei gleichbleibender Motorleistung aus Gründen der Zuverlässigkeit kommt man vor allem im Umfeld der Reifen nicht klar. Am Ende der Saison kündigt Ferrari die Geschäftsverbindung mit Firestone auf und baut bei letzten Tests bereits auf Pneus von Goodyear.

There was a touch of déjà-vu about the result of the German Grand Prix in 1972. It was won by Jacky Ickx, with Clay Regazzoni as runner-up, both in Ferraris – like at Zeltweg in 1970. But in the 1972 season the Scuderia had to make do with that single success. It had required the combined efforts of two outstanding drivers at the Nürburgring, which in those days was rightfully called the most beautiful and difficult race track in the world. Apart from their spectacular German achievement, podium finishes were rare for the unequal couple; two second places at Jarama and Monaco and a third at Buenos Aires for Ickx, third position for Regazzoni in Spain. The 312/B2 still gave its fathers headaches. In terms of reliability, its performance was the same. But the tyre situation continued to be precarious. At the end of the season the business relationship with Firestone was discontinued. Instead, Goodyears were tested in final trials.

World Championship

Jarama (E), Clay Regazzoni

Nivelles (B), Clay Regazzoni

Monaco, Clay Regazzoni

Clermont-Ferrand (F), Giovanni „Nanni" Galli

1972

Clermont-Ferrand (F), Giovanni Galli

Nürburgring (D), Jacky Ickx leading

Nürburgring (D), Jacky Ickx, winner

Nürburgring (D), Jacky Ickx

Monza (I), Jacky Ickx

Monza (I), Jacky Ickx

1 1973 hat der 312/B2, gelenkt von Jacky Ickx und dem spindeldürren Arturo Merzario, sein Verfallsdatum entschieden überschritten. Sein Schöpfer Mauro Forghieri wird zu Heimarbeit in Maranello verknackt. Künftig fährt man zweigleisig: Nach einem weiteren Streik der italienischen Metallarbeiter lässt man das Aluminium-Monocoque bei dem englischen Spezialisten John Thompson fertigen, eine Idee, die gleichwohl von Ferrari-Ingenieur Alessandro Colombo angestoßen wird. Diese Version, die am Barceloneser Montjuich debütiert, bereitet der Scuderia wenig Freude und leitet den Abgang des ergrimmten Ickx auf Raten ein. Inzwischen heckt Forghieri den B3 Stufe 3 aus, von Merzario in Zeltweg im Alleingang präsentiert. Er nimmt die Zukunft vorweg mit seinem durchgehenden Spoiler vorn, dem gähnenden Lufteinlass hinter dem Sturzbügel und dem riesigen Flügel hinten, unterstützt von einer zentralen Säule.

19

In 1973 the 312/B2, driven by Jacky Ickx and spindly Italian Arturo Merzario, was well past its sell-by date. Its creator Mauro Forghieri briefly fell out of favour and had to do his homework at Maranello. Ferrari split its engineering effort in two. After yet another metal workers' strike, the marque had its first aluminium monocoque built by English specialist John Thompson. Recent acquisition Alessandro Colombo was credited with that idea, which revealed a completely new approach. The variant was used from the Spanish Grand Prix at Montjuich, affording little pleasure and leading to the phased desertion of the Scuderia's former ace driver Jacky Ickx. In the meantime, Forghieri had refined the Tipo 312/B3 into a mark 3 version, which was driven by Merzario at Zeltweg, while Ickx was sitting out the race. It presented the first one-piece front and a huge rear wing supported by a single pillar, as well as an enormous air scoop above the rollover bar, the start of things to come.

World Championship

Monza (I), Jacky Ickx

Monaco, Arturo Merzario

Anderstorp (S), Jacky Ickx

Monza (I), Jacky Ickx

Im Juni 1973 macht Enzo Ferrari Luca di Montezemolo, den 25-jährigen Protégé des Fiat-Häuptlings Gianni Agnelli, zu seinem Assistenten. Mit drei Maßnahmen beweist der elegante Bologneser Marquis umgehend eine glückliche Hand: Er erhebt Mauro Forghieri wieder auf seinen angestammten Platz als technischer Direktor, heuert die vorjährigen BRM-Piloten Clay Regazzoni und Niki Lauda und begradigt die Fronten. Denn die Rennsportwagen der Marke, in die sich die Gestione Sportiva verzettelt hat, werden aufs Altenteil geschoben. Forghieri sublimiert den 312/B3 zum Sieger, wenn man auch zunächst noch mit einer Anzahlung auf künftigen Erfolg vorlieb nehmen muss. Di Montezemolo und der junge Lauda finden sich umgehend zu einer formidablen Verbindung zusammen. Seine neun Pole-Positions vermag der Österreicher indessen lediglich in die beiden Siege von Jarama und Zandvoort umzumünzen. Regazzoni empfiehlt sich mit einem Erfolg am Nürburgring.

19

In June 1973, Enzo Ferrari brought in Luca di Montezemolo, the 25-year-old protégé of Fiat supremo Gianni Agnelli, as his assistant. The elegant Bolognese marquis instantly made his presence felt with three measures. He brought Mauro Forghieri back into his accustomed position as technical director. He re-hired Clay Regazzoni and signed Niki Lauda, who had partnered the popular Swiss at BRM the year before. And he focused the efforts of the Gestione Sportiva on Formula 1 by canning the distracting sports car programme. Forghieri honed the 312/B3 into a winner, though he had to content himself with a down payment for future success. Di Montezemolo and young Lauda instantaneously gelled into a formidable combination. The Austrian took nine poles, but circumstances conspired to restrict him to just two wins at Jarama and Zandvoort. Regazzoni overcame the sternest challenge of the season winning at the Nürburgring.

World Championship

1 Emerson Fittipaldi (55)
2 Clay Regazzoni (52)
3 Jody Scheckter (45)
4 Niki Lauda (38)
5 Ronnie Peterson (35)
6 Carlos Reutemann (32)
7 Denny Hulme (20)
8 James Hunt (15)
9 Patrick Depailler (14)
10 Jacky Ickx (12)
10 Mike Hailwood (12)
12 Carlos Pace (11)
13 Jean-Pierre Beltoise (10)
14 Jean-Pierre Jarier (6)
14 John Watson (6)
16 Hans-Joachim Stuck (5)
17 Arturo Merzario (4)
18 Graham Hill (1)
18 Tom Pryce (1)
18 Vittorio Brambilla (1)

Jarama (E), Niki Lauda, winner

Zandvoort (NL), Niki Lauda 1st, Clay Regazzoni 2nd, Emerson Fittipaldi 3rd

1974

Zandvoort (NL), Niki Lauda

Monaco, Clay Regazzoni leading Niki Lauda

Anderstorp (S), Clay Regazzoni

Brand Hatch (GB), Niki Lauda with "flat tyre"

Nürburgring (D) Regazzoni siegt am Ring vor Scheckter, während Pole-Mann Lauda kurz nach dem Start durch Kollision mit dessen Tyrrell aussche

Nürburgring (D) Regazzoni won at the "Ring" from Scheckter, with whose Tyrrell pole-man Lauda collided approaching the second corner.

Monza (I), Niki Lauda

W as im Jahr zuvor bereits angeklungen ist, verdichtet sich nun zum Ereignis. 1975 wird zum Jahr der Zwölfzylinder aus Maranello. Nach elf Jahren Askese in Sachen Erfolg prasseln die Siege auf Ferrariland herab wie warmer Regen. Erneut radiert Niki Lauda neun Pole-Positions auf die Pisten des Grand-Prix-Zyklus. Der Österreicher gewinnt in Monaco, Zolder, Anderstorp, Le Castellet und Watkins Glen. Seine erste Weltmeisterschaft ist schon ab Monza nicht mehr zu erschüttern. Dort muss er indessen seinem Teamkollegen Regazzoni den Vortritt lassen. Wie 1970 feiern die tifosi den Mann aus dem Schweizer Mendrisio, als sei er einer von ihnen. Der beiden verlässliches Sportgerät vom dritten Lauf in Kyalami an, in Fiorano bis zum Abwinken ausgetestet: Mauro Forghieris Meisterstück 312 T. Das T (= trasversale) steht für die Position des Getriebes quer vor der Hinterachse, das eine bessere Massenkonzentration zum Schwerpunkt hin begünstigt.

19

T he potential that had begun to show the year before was now fully realised. In 1975 the flat-twelve cars from Maranello proved to be the class of the field. After more than a decade of abstention from success, victories pattered down on Ferrari country like warm rain. Niki Lauda took another nine poles, winning for the Prancing Stallion at Monaco, Zolder, Anderstorp, Le Castellet and Watkins Glen. His first championship was firmly under his belt as early as Monza. In the Royal Park, however, he had to let his team mate Regazzoni go first. Like 1970, the tifosi celebrated the man from Mendrisio, near Lugano, as though he came right from their midst. From the third race of the season at Kyalami, the pair's reliable tool was Mauro Forghieri's masterpiece the 312/T, extensively tested on the Ferrari home track at Fiorano. The T (=trasversale) stood for the transverse gearbox inside the wheelbase of the model, reducing polar moments of inertia.

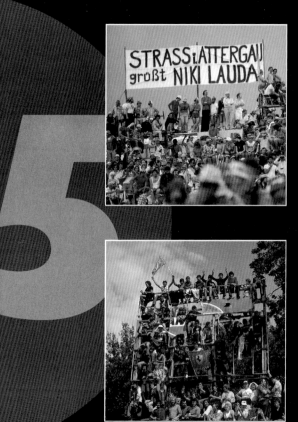

World Championship

1 Niki Lauda (64.5)
2 Emerson Fittipaldi (45)
3 Carlos Reutemann (37)
4 James Hunt (33)
5 Clay Regazzoni (25)
6 Carlos Pace (24)
7 Jody Scheckter (20)
7 Jochen Mass (20)
9 Patrick Depailler (12)
10 Tom Pryce (8)
11 Vittorio Brambilla (6.5)
12 Jacques Laffite (6)
12 Ronnie Peterson (6)
14 Mario Andretti (5)
15 Mark Donohue (4)
16 Jacky Ickx (3)
17 Alan Jones (2)
18 Jean-Pierre Jarier (1.5)
19 Tony Brise (1)
19 Gijs van Lennep (1)
21 Lella Lombardi (0.5)

Montjuich (E), Clay Regazzoni

Monaco, Niki Lauda, winner

Anderstorp (S), Niki Lauda, winner

Nürburgring (D)

Nürburgring (D), Niki Lauda

Zeltweg (A), Clay Regazzoni

Schon fünf erste Plätze hat Niki Lauda 1976 angehauft, in Brasilien, Südafrika, Belgien, Monaco und England, da grinst am Nürburgring der Renntod über die Leitplanke. Ein schwerer Unfall endet in einem Feuerball. Man zweifelt an seinem Aufkommen. Aber in Monza sechs Wochen später sitzt Lauda wieder im Wagen wie ein Phantom und versucht, sein werdendes zweites Championat gegen den anstürmenden McLaren-Helden James Hunt zu verteidigen. Das misslingt. Denn im grauen Regen des Finales in Fuji meldet sich mächtig sein Unterbewusstes zu Wort und er steigt vorzeitig aus. Enzo Ferrari rast. Auch Regazzoni hält die Fahne mit dem schwarzen Pferd hoch: Pole-Position, Start-Ziel-Sieg und schnellste Runde in Long Beach. Bis zu diesem Lauf muss noch der 312 T herhalten. Ab Jarama bestreitet man die Saison mit dem T2 und verbeugt sich damit vor den neuen Regeln: kein großer Lufteinlass mehr und 20 Zentimeter Überhang weniger für den Heckflügel.

In 1976, Niki Lauda had already amassed the five victories in Brazil, South Africa, Belgium, Monaco and England when, at the Nürburgring, the Grim Reaper grinned over the Armco. In an enormous accident the Austrian's Ferrari exploded in a fireball. His recovery seemed doubtful. But six weeks later, at Monza, he was sitting in his car again like a phantom, trying to defend his nascent second title against the onslaught of McLaren hero James Hunt. His heroics came to nought. In the grey rains of the Fuji finale his subconscious prevailed and Lauda climbed out of his car after two laps. Enzo Ferrari was livid. Clay Regazzoni was rarely as quick, but kept the Ferrari flag flying by taking pole, leading all the way and setting fastest lap at Long Beach. Until then, the preceding year's 312/T had still been going strong. The second-generation T2 appeared at Jarama, in keeping with the new rules that eliminated large

World Championship

1 James Hunt (69)
2 Niki Lauda (68)
3 Jody Scheckter (49)
4 Patrick Depailler (39)
5 Clay Regazzoni (31)
6 Mario Andretti (22)
7 John Watson (20)
7 Jacques Laffite (20)
9 Jochen Mass (19)
10 Gunnar Nilsson (11)
11 Ronnie Peterson (10)
11 Tom Pryce (10)
13 Hans-Joachim Stuck (8)
14 Carlos Pace (7)
14 Alan Jones (7)
16 Carlos Reutemann (3)
16 Emerson Fittipaldi (3)
18 Chris Amon (2)
19 Rolf Stommelen (1)
19 Vittorio Brambilla (1)

Long Beach (USA), Clay Regazzoni, winner

Long Beach (USA), Clay Regazzoni

Le Castellet (F), Niki Lauda

Monaco, Niki Lauda, winner

Long Beach (USA), Niki Lauda

Le Castellet (F), Clay Regazzoni

Le Castellet (F), Niki Lauda

Nürburgring (D), Clay Regazzoni, Niki Lauda

Nürburgring (D), Niki Lauda

Nürburgring (D), 2nd start

Lieber Niki«, schreibt Enzo Ferrari an den Österreicher, nachdem ihm dieser zu Jody Scheckters Championat 1979 gratuliert hat, »Dein Telegramm löste in mir Bitternis aus. Wäre Niki Lauda bei Ferrari geblieben, hätte er Fangios Rekord bereits eingestellt.« Die Hypothese zeugt von einem erstaunlichen Rechenfehler und von später Trauer. Zwar genügen Lauda die drei Siege in Kyalami, Hockenheim und Zandvoort zu seiner zweiten Weltmeisterschaft. Zwar stellt der 312/T2 unter Beweis, dass in jenen Jahren ein gutes Design durchaus noch für eine zweite Saison taugt. Indes: Zwei Rennen stehen noch aus, da rebelliert er gegen den Alten von Maranello und geht. Vor allem ist er erbost über die Art und Weise, in der Regazzoni geschasst und an seiner Statt Carlos Reutemann eingestellt wurde. Auch Luca di Montezemolo ist zu neuen Ufern aufgebrochen. Verstöße gegen den Grundsatz »Never change a winning team« taten schon immer weh.

19

Dear Niki", was Enzo Ferrari's answer to the Austrian after he had congratulated him on Jody Scheckter's 1979 title, "your telegram brought a bitter thought to my mind: if Lauda had stayed with Ferrari, he would have already matched Fangio's record." That assumption betrayed an amazing arithmetical error as well as somewhat belated grief. After all, Lauda's three victories at Kyalami, Hockenheim and Zandvoort earned him a second title. And the 312/T2 proved the point that, in those days, a good design could survive for more than just one season. But with two races to go, Lauda rebelled against the awe-inspiring Old Man from Maranello and called it quits. He was particularly unimpressed with the way Clay Regazzoni had been fired and Carlos Reutemann had been hired. Luca di Montezemolo had also left, to join the higher echelons of the Fiat hierarchy. It just does not pay to infringe the time-honoured principle "Never change a winning team."

Long Beach (USA), Niki Lauda, Carlos Reutemann

Nach dem Start in Long Beach (USAW) müssen Reutemann (Ferrari) und andere in den Notausgang.

After the start in Long Beach (USAW), Reutemann (Ferrari) and others had to resort to the emergency exit.

Long Beach (USA), Niki Lauda

Hockenheim (D), Chief Mechanic Cuoghi, Niki Lauda

Hockenheim (D), Niki Lauda

Hockenheim (D), Niki Lauda, winner

Hockenheim (D), Stuck 3rd, Niki Lauda 1st, Scheckter 2nd

Dijon-Prenois (F), Carlos Reutemann

Monza (I), Niki Lauda

Zeltweg (A), Niki Lauda, leading from pole

Mit dem 312/T3 von 1978 verfügt man erneut über ein vorzügliches Auto. Als hilfreich erweist sich zudem der Deal mit Neueinsteiger Michelin: Dessen Radialreifen mit ihrer breiten Auflagefläche vertragen sich prächtig mit dem Chassis des T3 und müssen lediglich mit Renault geteilt werden. Auch bewährt sich eine Fahrer-Combo, wie sie unterschiedlicher nicht hätte ausfallen können. Der enigmatische Argentinier Carlos Reutemann hat bereits sechs Grand-Prix-Jahre auf dem Buckel. An seiner Seite tobt seit dem Großen Preis von Kanada in Mosport 1977 an der Stürmer und Dränger Gilles Villeneuve. Der Commendatore wird ihn bald fast zärtlich seinen »kleinen Prinzen der Zerstörung« nennen. Gemeinsam schlägt man sich beachtlich gegen die Aufsteigergeneration der Wing Cars vom Schlage des Lotus 79. Reutemann gewinnt die Grands Prix von Brasilien, USA West und Ost und England, Villeneuve seinen ersten von insgesamt sechs für die Scuderia im heimischen Kanada.

19

The 312/T3 of 1978 was another superb car in the flat-twelve and transverse gearbox tradition of the seventies. Moreover, Ferrari took full advantage of a deal with newcomer Michelin, whose radial tyres with their greater tread contact area got along well with the T3's chassis and had to be shared only with Renault. In terms of the drivers, the Scuderia adjusted to life without Lauda with two characters who could not have been more different. The enigmatic Argentinian Carlos Reutemann already looked back on six Formula 1 years. From the 1977 Canadian Grand Prix at Mosport, exuberant Gilles Villeneuve was winning the hearts of his fans with his press-on attitude. The Commendatore would soon call him his "little prince of destruction", almost tenderly. The pair held their own impressively against the new generation of ground-effect cars such as the Lotus 79. Reutemann won the Brazilian, the British and the two US Grands Prix. Villeneuve scored his first of a total of six Ferrari wins in his native Canada.

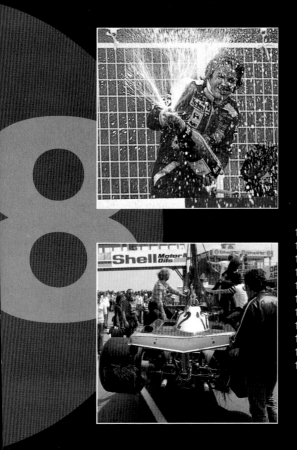

World Championship

Le Castellet (F), Carlos Reutemann, Gilles Villeneuve

Brands Hatch (GB), Carlos Reutemann

Hockenheim (D), Gilles Villeneuve

Brands Hatch (GB), Villeneuves car after crash in practice

Brands Hatch (GB), Carlos Reutemann, winner

Brands Hatch (GB), Carlos Reutemann

1978

Zeltweg (A), Carlos Reutemann

Zeltweg (A), Gilles Villeneuve

Zeltweg (A), Gilles Villeneuve, 1st podium, 3rd place

Eigentlich taugen die Ferrari T-Modelle der späten Siebziger mit ihren breit bauenden Zwölf-zylinder-Boxern nicht zum aktuellen Wing Car, das sich auf Grund der raffinierten Ausfor-mung seines Unterbodens an der Fahrbahn festsaugt wie eine Nacktschnecke. Vielmehr kommt das Prinzip Ground Effect dem kleinen und kompakten DFV-V8 von Ford entgegen, der den Piloten der Rivalen im Nacken sitzt. Nur: 1979 ist der Vorjahressieger Lotus aus dem Tritt gera-ten, Ligier und Williams haben noch nicht richtig Tritt gefasst. In dieses Vakuum platziert die Scuderia die Ausbaustufe T4 mit ihren sorgfältig geführten Luftströmen als das beste Paket. Wie einst der 156/F1 ist der 312/T4 der geborene Gewinner. Reutemann ist zu Lotus abgewandert. An seiner Stelle sitzt der bärige Südafrikaner Jody Scheckter im roten Cockpit, loyal unterstützt von Gilles Villeneuve, obwohl der häufig der Schnellere ist. Mit jeweils drei Siegen werden die beiden Champion und Vize. Das muss lange reichen.

19

The wing cars of the late seventies clung to the ground like slugs because of the sophisti-cated configuration of their underbodies. Doubtless, the Ferrari T-models with their wide twelve cylinder boxer engines were far from being cut out to comply with that principle. Instead, it flattered the small and compact Ford DFV V8s installed in the engine bays of their toughest competitors. But in 1979, the once all-conquering Lotuses fell out of step, whereas Ligier and Williams had not got into step yet. Into that vacuum, the Scuderia placed the 312/T Mark 4 with its carefully researched and guided internal flows as the best package. Like the leg-endary 1961 156/F1 model, the 312/T4 was a go-getter. Reutemann had defected to Lotus. In lieu of him, the burly South African Jody Scheckter sat in the red car's cockpit, loyally support-ed by Gilles Villeneuve, although the little man from Quebec was often the quicker. The two became champion and runner-up, with three victories each. That had to suffice for a long time.

World Championship

1 **Jody Scheckter (51)**
2 **Gilles Villeneuve (47)**
3 Alan Jones (40)
4 Jacques Laffite (36)
5 Clay Regazzoni (29)
6 Patrick Depailler (20)
6 Carlos Reutemann (20)
8 René Arnoux (17)
9 John Watson (15)
10 Didier Pironi (14)
10 J.P. Jarier (14)
10 Mario Andretti (14)
13 Jean-Pierre Jabouille (9)
14 Niki Lauda (4)
15 Nelson Piquet (3)
15 Elio de Angelis (3)
15 Jacky Ickx (3)
15 Jochen Mass (3)
19 Riccardo Patrese (2)
19 Hans-Joachim Stuck (2)
21 Emerson Fittipaldi (1)

Long Beach (USA), start

Jarama (E), Gilles Villeneuve

1979

Jarama (E), Gilles Villeneuve

Monaco, Jody Scheckter, winner, leading Gilles Villeneuve

1979

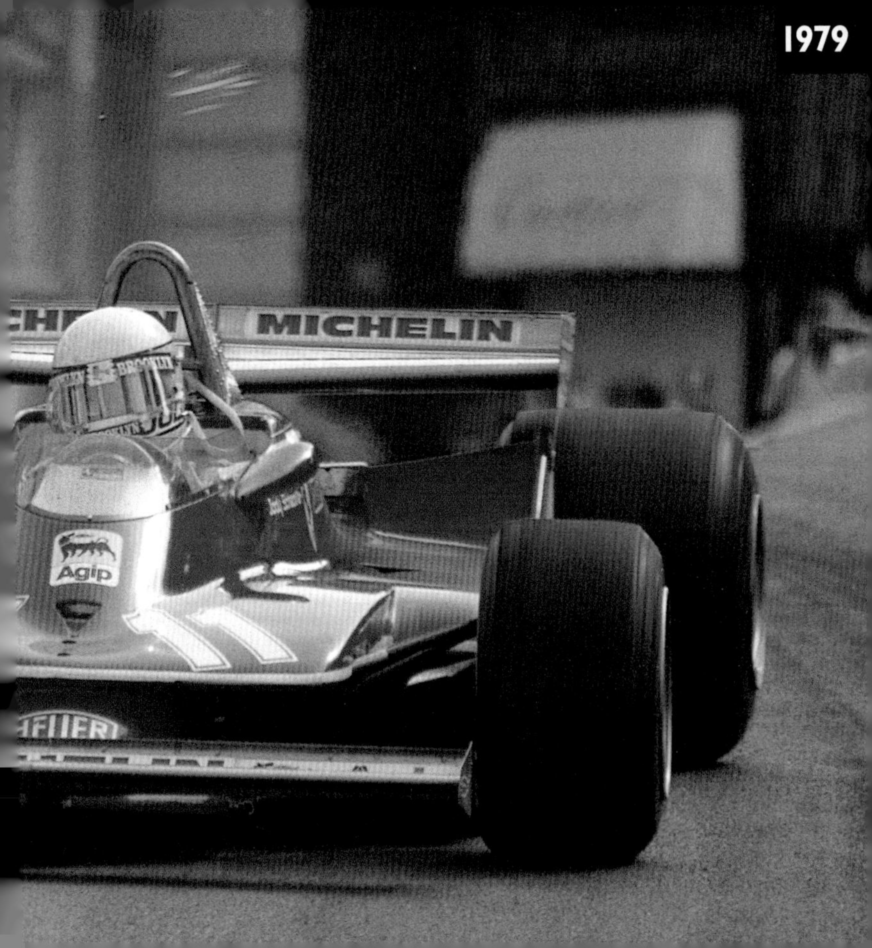

Monza (I), Gilles Villeneuve

1979

Monaco, Jody Scheckter

Hockenheim (D), Jody Scheckter

Zeltweg (A), Gilles Villeneuve

Zeltweg (A), Gilles Villeneuve, leading

Der Jubel des Vorjahres ist noch nicht verklungen, da kommt Jammer auf: Die Gilles-und-Jody-Show verkümmert zur Farce. Kein Sieg mag sich mehr für die beiden am Lenkrad des 312/T5 einstellen. Schlimmer noch: Der Frankokanadier landet mit vier anderen auf Platz zehn der Bestenliste, der Südafrikaner auf Position 19. Ferrari verkriecht sich in der Endwertung der Konstrukteure auf einem schmählichen zehnten Rang noch hinter Armeleuteteams wie Arrows und Fittipaldi. Am Ende der Saison hängt Jody Scheckter entmutigt seinen Sturzhelm an den Nagel. Den Biss, der ihn berühmt gemacht hat, hat er schon vorher verloren. Was ist geschehen? Die Ferrari 312/T haben am Ausgang einer beispiellosen Karriere ihr Pulver verschossen. Mit dem T5 rollt am Ende auch der legendäre flache Zwölfzylinder in den Ruhestand. Um den Bodeneffekt zu verstärken, hat man sogar an seinen Maßen gearbeitet. Immerhin vier Zentimeter schmaler sind seine neuen Zylinderköpfe – vergeblich.

No sooner had the rejoicing of the year before died down than wailing and gnashing of teeth prevailed in Maranello. The Gilles-and-Jody show had become a farce. There was no victory for the two and the Ferrari 312/T5 in 1980. Worse still: together with four others, the Franco-Canadian was reduced to a poor tenth position in the final results, the South African to a humiliating 19th. In the constructors' championship, Ferrari ended up a distant tenth, even behind notorious backbenchers such as Arrows and Fittipaldi. At the end of the season Jody Scheckter hung up his helmet for good, disheartened. The flamboyance that had been his trademark had long gone. What had happened? The 312/T had wound up its distinguished career in a miserable way. Together with the T5, the legendary flat-twelve was pensioned off. To improve ground effect, even its dimensions had been cut down, with new cylinder heads four centimetres narrower – in vain.

World Championship

Long Beach (USA), Jody Scheckter

Long Beach (USA), Gilles Villeneuve

1980

Monaco, Jody Scheckter

Zandvoort (NL), Jody Scheckter

1980

Brands Hatch (GB), Gilles Villeneuve

Zandvoort (NL), Jody Scheckter

1980

Imola (I), Gilles Villeneuve with the new turbo car in practice

Seine Aufwartung macht der Ferrari 126 C beim Training zum Gran Premio d'Italia 1980 in Imola. Gilles Villeneuve erzielt mit ihm die achtbeste Zeit. Zur Kunst, Ferrari-Kürzel richtig zu deuten, bedarf es wieder einmal der Interpretation durch den Künstler selbst. In das hastig angepasste Chassis des T5 eingepflanzt, verrichtet im 126 C ein V6 mit dem Gabelwinkel von 120 Grad mit dumpfem Posaunen seinen Dienst. Die Scuderia ist dem Beispiel des Konkurrenten Renault gefolgt. Im weiten Tal zwischen den Zylinderbänken setzen zwei Turbolader den 1,5-Liter-Sechszylinder unter Druck. Lieferant ist KKK, deshalb für 1981 der Zusatz K im Modellnamen. Neu im Team ist Didier Pironi. Die beiden Siege jenes Jahres muss er indessen dem Frankokanadier überlassen. In Monaco rührt Villeneuve mit einer Mischung von Glück und Wagemut einen wahren Hexenkessel auf. Ebenso spektakulär fährt er in Jarama. Da kommt keiner an dem kleinen Mann vorbei – buchstäblich.

The Ferrari 126 C was given its first public airing during practice for the 1980 Italian Grand Prix at Imola. Gilles Villeneuve was eighth fastest in it. As so often with Ferraris, the model's name did not necessarily speak for itself: Implanted into the hastily adapted chassis of the T5, a V6 with a bank angle of 120 degrees was at work, uttering a muffled trombone sound. The Scuderia had followed the example of Renault. In the wide valley between the two cylinder banks were positioned two turbochargers. They were provided by KKK, hence the K added to the 1981 model code. Jody Scheckter had been replaced by Didier Pironi. The two victories of that year were, however, notched up by the Franco-Canadian. At Monaco, Villeneuve sent his numerous fans into raptures with a mixture of luck, bravery and skill. He was every bit as spectacular at Jarama, where nobody was able to pass the little man – almost literally, as his 126/CK was particularly wide that day.

World Championship

1 Nelson Piquet (50)
2 Carlos Reutemann (49)
3 Alan Jones (46)
4 Jacques Laffite (44)
5 Alain Prost (43)
6 John Watson (27)
7 Gilles Villeneuve (25)
8 Elio de Angelis (14)
9 René Arnoux (11)
9 Hector Rebaque (11)
11 Riccardo Patrese (10)
11 Eddie Cheever (10)
13 Didier Pironi (9)
14 Nigel Mansell (8)
15 Bruno Giacomelli (7)
16 Marc Surer (4)
17 Mario Andretti (3)
18 Patrick Tambay (1)
18 Andrea de Cesaris (1)
18 Slim Borgudd (1)
18 Eliseo Salazar (1)

Imola (RSM), Gilles Villeneuve, Didier Pironi

Long Beach (USA), Villeneuve, start, missing 1st corner

Imola (RSM), Gilles Villeneuve

Dijon-Prenois (F), Gilles Villeneuve

Imola (RSM), Gilles Villeneuve, leading

Monaco, Gilles Villeneuve, winner

Hockenheim (D), Gilles Villeneuve

Zandvoort (NL), Gilles Villeneuve spun off at start

Monaco, Didier Pironi

Das Manko der Baureihe 126 bislang: Ihr Fahrwerk hat nicht Schritt gehalten mit dem bärenstarken Turbo-Triebwerk. Man heuert 1981 den englischen Chassis-Guru Doktor Harvey Postlethwaite an. Der verordnet dem Modell ein Monocoque aus Kompositmaterialien. Das quer angeordnete Fünfganggetriebe ist schmaler geworden. In puncto Abtrieb zählt der 126/C2 zu den Besten in der Branche. Pfeilschnell ist er auch. Mit kühlender Wassereinspritzung und verbessertem elektronischem Management macht sich der V6 in der Qualifikation über 750 PS stark. Das bedeutet 346 Stundenkilometer auf den Geraden von Le Castellet und Zeltweg. Gleichwohl wird 1982 ein schlimmes Ferrari-Jahr. Villeneuve kommt in Zolder ums Leben. Pironi wird nach einem schweren Unfall in Hockenheim zum Frührentner. Patrick Tambay und Mario Andretti springen ein. Als am Ende zusammengezählt wird, bleibt nur der Titel bei den Konstrukteuren.

The most obvious weakness of the Tipo 126 so far had been that its chassis was not on a par with its strong turbo engine. So Ferrari hired English specialist Dr. Harvey Postlethwaite. He prescribed the model the first monocoque of composite materials. The transverse gearbox had become narrower. In terms of ground effect, the 126/C2 was among the best in the business. It was also ultrafast. With water injection cooling its innards and advanced electronics, the output of the V6 exceeded 750 bhp in qualifying trim. On the straights of Le Castellet and Zeltweg, the car reached a breathtaking 346 kph. But nevertheless 1982 turned out to be a bad year for the Scuderia. Ferrari hero and all-time great Gilles Villeneuve died at Zolder. Pironi's career came to a sudden end when he crashed at Hockenheim, as he looked destined to take the title. Patrick Tambay and Mario Andretti did a fine job to secure the constructors' crown. In the final drivers' standings, Pironi was still second…

World Championship

1 Keke Rosberg (44)
2 Didier Pironi (39)
2 John Watson (39)
4 Alain Prost (34)
5 Niki Lauda (30)
6 René Arnoux (28)
7 Patrick Tambay (25)
7 Michele Alboreto (25)
9 Elio de Angelis (23)
10 Riccardo Patrese (21)
11 Nelson Piquet (20)
12 Eddie Cheever (15)
13 Derek Daly (8)
14 Nigel Mansell (7)
15 Carlos Reutemann (6)
15 Gilles Villeneuve (6)
17 Andrea de Cesaris (5)
17 Jacques Laffite (5)
19 Mario Andretti (4)
20 Jean-Pierre Jarier (3)
20 Marc Surer (3)
22 Manfred Winkelhock (2)
22 Eliseo Salazar (2)
22 Bruno Giacomelli (2)
22 Mauro Baldi (2)
26 Chico Serra (1)

Long Beach (USA), Didier Pironi

Long Beach (USA), Gilles Villeneuve, 3rd, but later disqualified

1982

Long Beach (USA), Gilles Villeneuve

Zolder (B), Gilles Villeneuve

Tod eines Giganten: Villeneuve stirbt in Zolder (B) bei der Qualifikation.

Death of a giant: Villeneuve was killed at Zolder (B) during qualification.

Monaco, Didier Pironi

Brands Hatch (GB), Niki Lauda (left) winner, Didier Pironi 2nd, Patrick Tambay 3rd

Hockenheim (D), Patrick Tambay, winner

Kuriosum 1983: Die Piloten der Scuderia verkehren miteinander muttersprachlich – auf Französisch. Sie heißen Patrick Tambay und René Arnoux und erneuern bei Ferrari ihre Formel-2-Partnerschaft von 1976 im Dienst von Martini-Renault. Der C3, die dritte Generation der Turbo-Baureihe 126, ist ein gutes Auto. Erstmalig besteht sein Chassis aus Kohlefaser und Kevlar, zwei Halbschalen, die auf der horizontalen Ebene verklebt und verschraubt sind. Hintere Finnen sollen erneut Abtrieb erzeugen, nachdem die FIA der Formel 1 flache Bäuche verschrieben und die auf der Fahrbahn schleifenden seitlichen Schürzen verbannt hat. In der zweiten Hälfte der Saison siegt Arnoux in Montreal, Hockenheim und Zandvoort. Nach Monza liegt er nur zwei Punkte hinter Tabellenführer Prost. Doch die verbleibenden beiden Rennen missraten zu Flops: nur Rang neun und eine Runde zurück in Brands Hatch, Ausfall in Kyalami, Platz eins für die Roten nur bei den Konstrukteuren – wie gehabt.

A 1983 curiosity: the two drivers were native French speakers. As Ferrari employees they renewed their successful 1976 Formula 2 partnership in the services of Martini-Renault. Without doubt, the C3, third link in the evolutionary chain of turbo-propelled Tipo 126 models, was a good car. For the first time its chassis consisted of carbon fibre and Kevlar, two half shells glued and screwed together along the horizontal plane. Rear fins were to look after maximum possible downforce since the FIA had imposed upon Formula 1 the flat bottom rule as well as banning skirts. In the second half of the season Arnoux notched up victories at Montreal, Hockenheim and Zandvoort. After Monza, he lay just two points behind championship leader Alain Prost but failed to deliver in the remaining two races, with ninth position one lap down at Brands Hatch and retirement at Kyalami. Again Ferrari had to be content with another constructors' title.

World Championship

200

Long Beach (USA), Patrick Tambay

Monaco, René Arnoux

1983

Monaco, René Arnoux

1983

Le Castellet (F), Patrick Tambay

Hockenheim (D), Andrea de Cesaris 3rd, René Arnoux 1st, Riccardo Patrese 2nd

Silverstone (GB), start, René Arnoux pole, Patrick Tambay 2nd

As Glied konsequenter Evolution mutiert der 126/C4 aus dem Modell des Vorjahres. Noch ausgeprägter zeigt sich seine Pfeilform, da das Kühlsystem nach hinten verlagert worden ist. Ein anderer Schwerpunkt bei seiner Konzeption: herunter mit den Pfunden. Mit 540 Kilogramm liegt der C4 erstmalig am erlaubten Mindestgewicht. In einer letzten Version mit längerem Radstand und einer sich verjüngenden Heckpartie à la McLaren werden diese Änderungen teilweise wieder zurückgenommen, als die Kühler wieder weiter vorn angesiedelt werden. Sie weist den Weg in die Zukunft und markiert zugleich das Ende der Ära Mauro Forghieri, der bei Ferrari noch eine Zeit lang anderen Verwendungen zugeführt wird. Viel richtet der 126/C4 nicht aus gegen die überaus starken McLaren-TAG/Porsche. Lediglich ein Sieg in der Sandwüste von Zolder ist zu verzeichnen, durch Michele Alboreto. Als erster italienischer Fahrer in der Scuderia seit über einem Jahrzehnt hat er Patrick Tambay beerbt.

The Ferrari 126/C4 looked an obvious successor to the preceding year's car. Its arrow shape was even more pronounced, as the cooling system had been shifted towards the rear end. Emphasis had also been placed on the reduction of excessive weight. With its 540 kg, the C4 was at the minimum allowed limit for the first time. In a final version, with longer wheelbase and McLaren-style tapering of the rear fairing, these changes were partly reversed as the radiators were moved forward again. It foreshadowed future designs but was also the final bow of Mauro Forghieri as technical director, as the vivacious Italian was in for another period at Ferrari in other jobs. In 1984 the McLaren and TAG/Porsche joint venture set the pace. Ferrari's only win was scored in the Zolder dustbowl by newcomer Michele Alboreto. The friendly little man from Milan was the first Italian signing to the Prancing Horse for more than a decade.

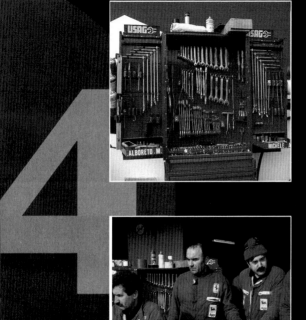

World Championship

Zolder (B), star

1984

Imola (RSM), Michele Alboreto

Monaco

Monaco, René Arnoux

Monaco, René Arnoux

Monza (I), René Arnoux

Monza (I), Michele Alboreto

Estoril (P), René Arnoux

Der veränderte Name zeigt es bereits: Der Tipo 156/85 ist ein völlig neues Auto. Sein Chassis ist vom Computer (CAD/CAM) ausgeheckt, die Aufhängung mit Zugstreben auf dem letzten Stand der Dinge, der Werkstoff für die Bremsscheiben Karbon. Voll ausgereift und von uriger Stärke, im Rennen bis zu 780 PS, bei der Qualifikation an die 950 PS, kommt der breite V6 ohne kühlende Wassereinspritzung aus. Die Turbolader, bislang in der Mulde zwischen dem V, siedeln nun unten seitlich. Selbst auf den anspruchsvollsten Kursen kann es der Ferrari 156/85 mit den McLaren MP4/2B-TAG aufnehmen, die in jenem Jahr das Feld beherrschen. Bei der Saison-Ouvertüre in Rio steht Alboreto auf Startplatz eins und verschafft sich mit guten Platzierungen sowie Siegen in Montreal und Hockenheim einen Vorsprung von fünf Zählern vor McLaren-Mann Alain Prost. Doch in der zweiten Hälfte des Zyklus hagelt es Ausfälle und Champion wird der Franzose.

Its different name shows that everything was indeed different: The Tipo 156/85 was a completely new car. Its body had been designed by computer (CAD/CAM) for the first time, with state-of-the-art pullrod suspension and carbon brake discs. The car's V6 unit, a mature piece of engineering and brutally strong with 780 bhp in race and up to 950 bhp in qualifying trim, no longer required water injection to cope with high temperatures. The turbochargers, once situated between the shanks of the wide V between the cylinder banks, had been shifted to a low lateral position. The 156/85 could cope with the all-conquering McLaren MP4/2B-TAGs on the most demanding tracks. Alboreto was on pole first time out in Rio. Scoring podium finishes in the first half of the season and winning at Montreal and Hockenheim, he emerged with a five-point-lead over McLaren's Alain Prost. But his challenge was blunted by an appalling run of failures in the second half and the Frenchman became champion.

World Championship

1 Alain Prost (73)
2 Michele Alboreto (53)
3 Keke Rosberg (40)
4 Ayrton Senna (38)
5 Elio de Angelis (33)
6 Nigel Mansell (31)
7 Stefan Johansson (26)
8 Nelson Piquet (21)
9 Jacques Laffite (16)
10 Niki Lauda (14)
11 Thierry Boutsen (11)
11 Patrick Tambay (11)
13 Marc Surer (5)
13 Derek Warwick (5)
15 Philippe Streiff (4)
15 Stefan Bellof (4)
17 René Arnoux (3)
17 Andrea de Cesaris (3)
17 Ivan Capelli (3)
17 Gerhard Berger (3)

Monaco, Michele Alboreto

1985

Monaco, Stefan Johansson

Monaco, Stefan Johansson

Le Castellet (F), Michele Alboreto

1985

Spa-Francorchamps (B), Michele Alboreto leading Stefan Johansson

D ie Saison 1986 mit Michele Alboreto und Stefan Johansson am Volant des F1-86 zeitigt nur dürftige Früchte. Der blonde Schwede arbeitet seit Estoril 1985 im Aufgebot der Scuderia – statt Arnoux, der nun wie so viele Ferrari-Verstoßene ins Nichts abdriften wird. Johanssons Bestes in der Saison 1986 sind vier dritte Plätze, während Alboretos Blütenträume mit einem zweiten, zwei vierten und einem fünften platzen. Im Championat der Konstrukteure sackt man auf Position vier ab, das magerste Ergebnis seit 1980. Schuld ist wohl das Mittelmaß des aktuellen Turbo-Projektils aus Maranello, das im Qualifikationstrimm gleichwohl mit bis zu 1050 PS auftrumpft. Es ist das vorerst letzte Werk des Dr. Harvey Postlethwaite für die Gestione Sportiva, der er seit 1981 angehört. Der Brite geht zur Tyrrell, sein Landsmann John Barnard kommt. Mit Billigung des Commendatore richtet er in England die Ferrari-Dependance GTO (für Guildford Technical Office) ein – ein Irrweg, wie sich zeigen wird.

T he 1986 season with Michele Alboreto and Stefan Johansson at the wheel of the F1-86 bore only poor fruit. The fair-haired Swede had been with the Scuderia since Estoril 1985, instead of Arnoux, who was in for the dour lot of most Ferrari refugees – oblivion. Johansson's best in the 1986 season was four third places, whereas Alboreto's fond hopes came to nought, with one second, two fourths and a fifth position. In the constructors' championship, Ferrari ended up a distant fourth, the outfit's worst placing since 1980. The frustrating lack of success was due to the obvious mediocrity of the current red turbo projectile, though its engine entered the 1000-plus bhp zone in qualifying. That year's car was Harvey Postlethwaite's last in spite of the Englishman's brief return in the early nineties. He left to join Tyrrell and John Barnard was hired. The Commendatore agreed to his setting up GTO (for Guildford Technical Office) as a remote Ferrari branch – an experiment that was to fail.

World Championship

1 Alain Prost (72)
2 Nigel Mansell (70)
3 Nelson Piquet (69)
4 Ayrton Senna (55)
5 Stefan Johansson (23)
6 Keke Rosberg (22)
7 Gerhard Berger (17)
8 Jacques Laffite (14)
8 Michele Alboreto (14)
8 René Arnoux (14)
11 Martin Brundle (8)
12 Alan Jones (4)
13 Johnny Dumfries (3)
13 Philippe Streiff (3)
15 Teo Fabi (2)
15 Patrick Tambay (2)
15 Riccardo Patrese (2)
18 Christian Danner (1)
18 Philippe Alliot (1)

Imola (RSM), Michele Alboreto

1986

Hungaroring (H), Stefan Johansson

Hockenheim (D). Stefan Johansson

Zeltweg (A), Michele Alboreto 2nd, Alain Prost, winner, Stefan Johansson 3rd

Zeltweg (A), Michele Alboreto

Ein allgemeines Stühlerücken bei Ferrari betrifft 1987 vor allem österreichische Bürger: Auf seinem kurzen Weg durch die Topteams wandert Johansson zu McLaren ab, Gerhard Berger rückt nach, von Benetton kommend. Der F1-87 stammt aus der Feder von Gustav Brunner, wird indessen nach den Weisungen des neuen technischen Direktors John Barnard verfeinert. Der Grazer verlässt die Scuderia anschließend, um ein Indycar zu bauen, das nie seiner Bestimmung zugeführt werden wird. Nach zwölf Jahren hat man das Getriebe wieder längs angebaut. Das kommt der Aerodynamik des roten Renners und dem Ground Effect zugute. Der Radstand wird mit 2800 mm um 34 mm länger, die Aufhängung durch die Verwendung besserer Federn optimiert, der Gabelwinkel des V6 auf 90 Grad reduziert. Dies sei, sagt Berger, der beste Ferrari, den er je gefahren habe. Spricht's – und revanchiert sich mit Siegen aus der Pole bei den letzten beiden Rennen in Japan und Australien.

A shift in Ferrari key personnel in 1987 mainly concerned Austrian citizens. On his brief way through the top teams, Swede Stefan Johansson defected to McLaren and was succeeded by Gerhard Berger of Benetton fame. The F1-87 had been conceived by Gustav Brunner but was fine-honed according to the instructions of new Technical Director John Barnard. Brunner departed when the design was ready in order to build an IndyCar that was never to race. After twelve years of sticking with the T-principle, the longitudinal arrangement of the gearbox was reinstated, improving the airflow hitting the red racer as well as restoring ground effect. The wheelbase was lengthened by 34 mm to 2,800 mm, the suspension of the car ameliorated by means of better springs, the angle between the banks of the V6 unit reduced to 90 degrees. Berger recalls the car as the best Ferrari he ever drove, showing his gratitude by winning the last two outings in Japan and Australia from pole.

World Championship

Monaco

Monaco, Michele Alboreto, Gerhard Berger

Monaco, Gerhard Berger

Monaco

1987

Hungaroring (H). Gerhard Berger

Zwei monumentale Startunfälle machen dem alten Österreichring (A) den Garaus. Gerhard Berger scheint ungerührt.
Two enormous start accidents spelled the end of the old Österreichring (A). Gerhard Berger seemed unaffected.

Jerez (E)

Jerez (E), Michele Alboreto

1987

Jerez (E), Michele Alboreto

D le Berger-Siege in Suzuka und Adelaide am Ende des Zyklus 1987 scheinen zu den schönsten Hoffnungen zu berechtigen. Aber der Schein trügt: 1988 missrät zum Übergangsjahr. Barnards opus 1, um den neuen V12-Saugmotor herum gebaut, sollte in der zweiten Hälfte der Saison in die Kampfhandlungen eingreifen. Es steht aber ab Juli lediglich für Tests zur Verfügung. So muss noch einmal das leicht angejahrte Turbo-Konzept herhalten. Es erweist sich als chancenlos vor dem Ansturm der McLaren MP4/4- Honda, die mit 15 Siegen in 16 Rennen den Rest der Grand-Prix-Welt zum Gespött machen. Eine Ausnahme bildet ausgerechnet Monza. Da stolpert das McLaren-Dreamteam. Alain Prost fällt aus, Ayrton Senna kommt sich mit dem Hinterbänkler Jean-Louis Schlesser ins Gehege. Die Scuderia stibitzt einen Doppelsieg, Berger vor Alboreto. Die tifosi frohlocken. Der Commendatore hingegen kann sich nicht mehr darüber freuen – er starb 14 Tage zuvor.

1988

T he momentum of Gerhard Berger's two wins at Suzuka and Adelaide at the end of the 1987 season did not carry on for long. Appearances were deceptive: 1988 was a year of transition. Barnard's opus no.1, built round the new normally aspirated V12 engine, had been scheduled to join the fray in the second half of the year. But it was available for test purposes only from July onwards. So the Scuderia had to resort to the slightly dated turbo concept. It was continually bested by the McLaren MP4/4-Honda package which made a mockery of the rest of the grand prix world, claiming 15 of the 16 races. The only one the dream team of Alain Prost and Ayrton Senna missed was Monza, where the Frenchman retired and the Brazilian collided with backmarker Jean-Louis Schlesser. So the Scuderia pilfered a one-two, Berger from Alboreto. The tifosi were delirious. The commendatore, however, could no longer join in the rejoicing. He had died a fortnight earlier.

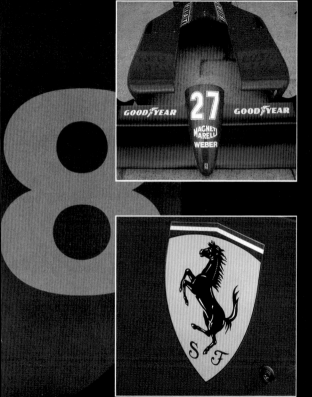

World Championship

1 Ayrton Senna (90)
2 Alain Prost (87)
3 Gerhard Berger (41)
4 Thierry Boutsen (27)
5 Michele Alboreto (24)
6 Nelson Piquet (22)
7 Ivan Capelli (17)
7 Derek Warwick (17)
9 Nigel Mansell (12)
9 Alessandro Nannini (12)
11 Riccardo Patrese (8)
12 Eddie Cheever (6)
13 Maurizio Gugelmin (5)
13 Jonathan Palmer (5)
15 Andrea de Cesaris (3)
16 Satoru Nakajima (1)
16 Pierluigi Martini (1)

Rio de Janeiro (BR), Gerhard Berger 2nd, Alain Prost, winner, Nelson Piquet 3rd

Rio de Janeiro (BR), Gerhard Berger

Monaco, Michele Alboreto

Silverstone (GB), start, Gerhard Berger, pole position, Michele Alboreto 2nd

Silverstone (GB), Gerhard Berger

Silverstone (GB), Michele Alboreto

1988

Monza (I), Michele Alboreto

Sie nennen ihn die Eierhandgranate. Denn die Rundungen von John Barnards Erstling F1-89 muten ebenso gefällig wie gefährlich an. Auch seine Lebenserwartung erinnert zuweilen an die seines militärischen Pendants nach dem Entfernen der Sicherung. Denn kurz und chaotisch war die Entwicklung des 3,5-Liter-V12 mit seinen Fünfventilköpfen, dessen melodischer Urschrei bei den Zuschauern gleichwohl Rauschzustände auslöst. Und als störanfällig erweist sich zunächst seine elektronische Siebengang-Automatik, schaltbar durch Paddel hinterm Lenkrad. Wie einst sein Karbonchassis bei McLaren zählt sie zu den Umstürzen, die Barnard in der Formel 1 angezettelt hat. Neuzugang Nigel Mansell gewinnt verblüfft seinen Einstand in Rio, muss sich jedoch sich für Triumph Nummer zwei bis Budapest gedulden. Berger übersteht einen Horrorcrash in Imola dank Gott und dem diamantharten Kunststoff-Kokon des F1-89 und siegt in Estoril. Das Championat bleibt McLaren-Sache.

The 1989 Ferrari weapon was officially called the F1-89 but soon dubbed the Mill's bomb as the curves of John Barnard's first-born looked both pleasing and dangerous. Sometimes its life expectancy, too, reminded one of its military counterpart after the safety pin had been removed. The development of its 3.5-litre unit with five-valve heads had been brief and chaotic, but the shrilly melodious cry of the V12 had the spectators lost in rapture. It was further hindered by the teething trouble of its electronic gearbox, the seven speeds being shifted by paddles behind the steering-wheel. Like Barnard's McLaren carbon-fibre chassis, it was to revolutionise the sport. Against all odds, Ferrari's new recruit Nigel Mansell won first time out in Rio but had to wait for triumph no. 2 until Budapest. Berger owed his survival in a horrific Imola crash to God and his diamond-hard composite monocoque. The Austrian went on to claim victory at Estoril. But it was McLaren that did most of the winning.

Monaco, Nigel Mansell

Rio de Janeiro (BR), Nigel Mansell, winner. Blood drops down from his finger, after a cut at the Trophy.

1989

Monaco, Nigel Mansell

Spa-Francorchamps (B), Gerhard Berger

Estoril (P), start, Gerhard Berger leading

Estoril (P), Gerhard Berger, winner

Estoril (P), podium

Estoril (P), Gerhard Berger, winner

Im Juni 1989 kündigt John Barnard an, er werde aus den Diensten der Scuderia ausscheren. Im Dauerzwist mit dem eigensinnigen Briten hat sich die italienische Fraktion bei Ferrari durchgesetzt. Zugleich winkt Hoffnung: Im Ringtausch mit Gerhard Berger hat man McLaren Alain Prost für sechs Millionen Dollar abspenstig gemacht. Der Franzose ist des zähen Ringens mit seinem Teamgefährten Senna überdrüssig und dürstet nach Taten. Zur Hand geht ihm dabei der Tipo 641, eine Hinterlassenschaft John Barnards, durch den Italo-Argentinier Enrique Scalabroni im Windkanal retuschiert. Seine Maschine gehört am Ende mit 720 PS zu den stärksten im ganzen Land. Mansell siegt in Estoril, der Franzose in den fünf Großen Preisen von Brasilien, Mexiko, Frankreich, England und Spanien. Er wird bis zum Finale in Suzuka als Titelaspirant gehandelt. Dort rammt ihn Erzfeind Senna in der ersten Kurve. Als sich der Staub des Kiesbetts gelegt hat, ist der Brasilianer Champion.

In June 1989, John Barnard announced that he was going to turn his back on the Scuderia. The Italian faction had won the continual war against the stubborn Briton. But hope was beckoning: Ferrari had seized one of McLaren's greatest assets exchanging Alain Prost for Gerhard Berger, to the tune of a six-million dollar salary for the Frenchman. He was fed up with the persistent feud with his team mate Senna and was thirsting for action. His mount was the Tipo 641 which had been left behind by John Barnard and aerodynamically retouched by the Italo-Argentinian, Enrique Scalabroni. At 720 bhp towards the end of the season, its engine was amongst the most powerful of all. Mansell won in Estoril, Prost in the five grands prix of Brazil, Mexico, France, Great Britain and Spain. Until the last race at Suzuka, he was a contender for the title. But then Senna deliberately rammed him in the first corner. When the gravel trap dust had settled, the Brazilian was champion.

World Championship

1 Ayrton Senna (78)
2 Alain Prost (71)
3 Nelson Piquet (43)
3 Gerhard Berger (43)
5 Nigel Mansell (37)
6 Thierry Boutsen (34)
7 Riccardo Patrese (23)
8 Alessandro Nannini (21)
9 Jean Alesi (13)
10 Ivan Capelli (6)
10 Roberto Moreno (6)
10 Aguri Suzuki (6)
13 Eric Bernard (5)
14 Derek Warwick (3)
14 Satoru Nakajima (3)
16 Stefano Modena (2)
16 Alex Caffi (2)
18 M. Gugelmin (1)

Hockenheim (D), Alain Prost

Spa-Francorchamps (B), Nigel Mansell

Spa-Francorchamps (B)

Jerez (E), Alain Prost, winner

Jerez (E), Alain Prost, Nigel Mansell 2nd

Le Castellet (F), Alain Prost, winner, Nigel Mansell

Imola (RSM)

An der Personalfront geht es 1991 stürmisch her: Piero Fusaro, glückloser Präsident der Firma, gibt den Stab an Luca di Montezemolo weiter. Harvey Postlethwaite kehrt ein zu einem kurzen Gastspiel. Monaco wird zum Waterloo von Rennleiter Cesare Fiorio. Seine Position nimmt Claudio Lombardi ein. Als Alain Prost seinen Arbeitgeber öffentlich verbellt, von jeher Sakrileg an der Sache Ferrari, kommt es zu Stunk und nach Suzuka zum Rausschmiss. Beim letzten Lauf in Adelaide startet an seiner Statt Gianni Morbidelli. Soviel Turbulenz bekommt der Sache nicht. Dem Barnard-Vermächtnis Tipo 642, von Steve Nichols sanft facegeliftet, folgt in Magny-Cours die neue Version 643, voll verdächtiger Ähnlichkeit zum Williams FW14. Die Bilanz bleibt dünn: drei Zweite und weniger für Prost, drei Dritte und weiterer Kleinkram für den Ferrari-Novizen Jean Alesi.

In 1991 Ferrari had to weather a stormy period due to a dramatic turnover of staff: Piero Fusaro, the hapless President, handed over to Luca di Montezemolo. Harvey Postlethwaite reappeared for a brief spell. The Monaco Grand Prix became the Waterloo of team manager Cesare Fiorio, who was replaced by Claudio Lombardi. Alain Prost ripped into his employer in public, a deadly sin since time immemorial. Trouble brewed and after Suzuka the Frenchman was fired. In the last race his place was filled by Gianni Morbidelli. All this was disastrous for the Ferrari cause. John Barnard's legacy the 642, slightly retouched by Steve Nichols, was succeeded by a completely new version named the 643 at Magny-Cours, obviously modelled upon the Williams FW14. The yield was poor: three second and lower placings for Prost, three thirds and some minor results for novice Jean Alesi.

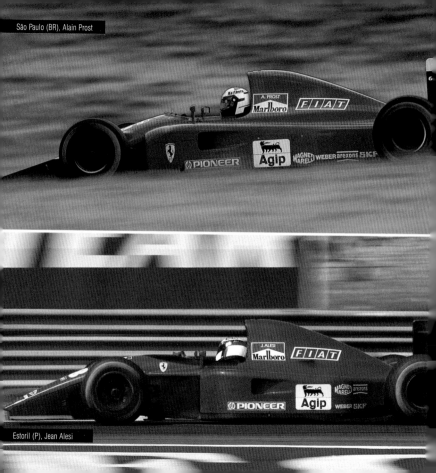

São Paulo (BR), Alain Prost

Estoril (P), Jean Alesi

Phoenix (USA)

Phoenix (USA), Jean Alesi pitstop

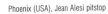

Phoenix (USA), Jean Alesi

Phoenix (USA), Jean Alesi

Monaco, Alain Prost

Monaco, Jean Alesi

Monaco, Jean Alesi

1992 kommt's noch schlimmer: Ferrari-Pilot Alesi wird nur Siebenter im Championat, Kollege in Rot und Spaßvogel Ivan Capelli lediglich Zwölfter. Der findet sich wegen anhaltender Erfolglosigkeit zwei Rennen vor Schluss zugunsten von Nicola Larini auf der Straße wieder. Schuld ist vor allem der F92A, entworfen von Steve Nichols und Jean-Claude Migeot und zweifellos schön. Attraktiv ist überdies das Ideengut, das in ihn eingebracht worden ist. Hinsichtlich der Aerodynamik haperte es bei den Vorgängern. Eine höhere Nase, ein vom Monocoque abgesetzter Unterboden, gotisch aufwachsende und etwas vom Rumpf abgesetzte Lufteinlässe sollen Abhilfe schaffen. Sechs Gänge, meinen seine Väter, dürften genügen. Mehr Bohrung und weniger Hub erzeugen höhere Drehzahlen und mehr Kraft. Gut in der Theorie, dürftig in der Praxis: Das gilt ebenso für den F92AT (mit Quergetriebe) ab Spa.

19

1992 was an even worse year. Jean Alesi found himself seventh in the final results, Ivan Capelli, his mate in the red livery and a tireless wag, was only twelfth. Because of persistent failure he lost his seat to Nicola Larini two races before the end. Above all, that was due to the deficiencies of the F92A, which had been conceived by Steve Nichols and Jean-Claude Migeot and was without doubt a beauty. Apart from that, it had been imbued with convincing ideas. Its predecessors had been dogged by aerodynamic problems. To sort those out, it was given a higher nose, an undertray separate from the chassis, tall and narrow air ducts at some distance from its trunk. Its makers had deemed that six gears were enough. More bore and less stroke translated into higher revs and increased power. But what was brilliant in theory did not work in practice. That also applied to the F92AT (with transverse gearbox) from Spa onwards.

World Championship

1 Nigel Mansell (108)
2 Riccardo Patrese (56)
3 Michael Schumacher (53)
4 Ayrton Senna (50)
5 Gerhard Berger (49)
6 Martin Brundle (38)
7 Jean Alesi (18)
8 Mika Hakkinen (11)
9 Andrea de Cesaris (8)
10 Michele Alboreto (6)
11 Erik Comas (4)
12 Karl Wendlinger (3)
12 Ivan Capelli (3)
14 Thierry Boutsen (2)
14 Pierluigi Martini (2)
14 Johnny Herbert (2)
17 Bertrand Gachot (1)
17 Christian Fittipaldi (1)
17 Stefano Modena (1)

Barcelona (E), Ivan Capelli, Jean Alesi

Estoril (P), Jean Alesi

Monaco

Mit Heimkehrer Gerhard Berger wird Jean Alesi 1993 ein starker Partner an die Seite gestellt. Doch wieder hapert's am Auto, dem F93A, dem Publikum ganz ungewöhnlich früh präsentiert, nämlich einen Tag vor Heiligabend 1992. Das Modell sei ein Lückenbüßer, räumt Designer Harvey Postlethwaite verschämt ein. Man warte auf die neueste Kreation von Heimkehrer John Barnard. Am Triebwerk liegt es nicht. Das rangiert mit seinen variablen Ansaugrohren und ursprünglich fünf, ab Hockenheim nur noch vier pneumatisch gesteuerten Ventilen je Zylinder und am Ende 750 PS unter den besten und stärksten, allerdings auch zu den durstigsten im Feld. Indes: Der F93A als erster und einziger Ferrari mit aktiver Aufhängung missrät zum rasenden Versuchslabor. Das Beste aus den 16 Läufen jenes Jahres: Rang zwei für Alesi in Monza, wo sonst. Ansonsten treibt Ferrari in einem Meer von Mittelmaß.

In 1993, Gerhard Berger was repatriated to Ferrari country, forming a strong pairing with Jean Alesi. But again the car did not keep up, although the F93A was presented to the public unusually early, namely one day before Christmas Eve 1992. It was just a stopgap, declared designer Harvey Postlethwaite bashfully. Everybody, he added, was waiting for the latest creation from John Barnard, yet another returnee. It was certainly not the fault of the engine. With its variable intake trumpets and pneumatic valves, at first five, from Hockenheim onwards only four per cylinder, and 750 bhp in its final version, it was among the best and the strongest in the field. But otherwise, the F93A, as the first and only Ferrari with active suspension, wasted away as a racing test laboratory. The best result of the 1993 season was Alesi's second place in Monza. Aside from that, Ferrari was floating in an ocean of mediocrity.

World Championship

São Paulo (BR), Jean Alesi

Monaco

1993

Hockenheim (D), Gerhard Berger

Montreal (CDN), Gerhard Berger

G. BERGER

Marlboro

FIAT

Agip

GOODYEAR

28

ONEER

Agip

MAGNETI MARELLI

SKF
arexons

BBS

Monza (I), Gerhard Berger

Hungaroring (H), Gerhard Berger

Hungaroring (H), Gerhard Berger 3rd

Magny-Cours (F), Jean Alesi

Barcelona (E), Jean Alesi

Im Juli 1993 hat sich der ehemalige Rallyebeifahrer und erfolgreiche Leiter des Peugeot-Sportprogramms Jean Todt angeschickt, das Gestrüpp von Egotrips zu roden, das die Befehlswege der Scuderia und die Zugänge zum Erfolg überwuchert. Aber gut Ding will Weile haben. Ein solches scheint John Barnards Tipo 412 T1 zu sein, überhäuft mit üppigem Vorschusslorbeer. Doch der welkt zügig im scharfen Wind der Realität. Die beiden ersten Rennen in Interlagos und Aida decken gnadenlos Design-Schnitzer auf, einen Mangel an aerodynamischer Ausgewogenheit und fiebrige Überhitzung des V12. Während Barnard frühzeitig in seiner englischen Denkfabrik in Klausur geht, um das Modell für 1995 auszuhecken, sublimiert sein Kollege Gustav Brunner in Maranello die Variante 412 T1B. Bergers Sieg in Hockenheim und eine erste Startreihe ganz in Rot in Monza sind der Lohn.

In July 1993, the former world-class rallye co-driver and successful boss of Peugeot's sporting activities, Jean Todt, set about clearing the brushwood of ego trips that overgrew the lines of command of the Scuderia and its paths to success. But a thing done well cannot be done quickly. John Barnard's Tipo 412 T1, upon which much premature praise was heaped, appeared to be promising indeed. Then all euphoria was scattered by the biting wind of reality. The first two races at Interlagos and Aida relentlessly uncovered basic design faults, a lack of aerodynamic balance and febrile engine overheating. Barnard soon disappeared into the seclusion of his think-tank back home in England to map out the 1995 model. In Maranello, his colleague Gustav Brunner evolved the existing car into its 412 T1B variant. His efforts were rewarded with Berger's victory in Hockenheim and a Ferrari-red front row at Monza.

Monza (I), Jean Alesi

Hockenheim (D), Gerhard Berger, winr

Magny-Cous (F), Jean Alesi

Magny-Cous (F)

Estoril (P), start

Estoril (P), Gerhard Berger

Am 6. Februar 1995 wird betont leger der 412 T2 vorgestellt, ein Bekenntnis von Star-Couturier John Barnard zu einfachen Formen und einfachen Lösungen. Für den leichten und kompakten V12, einen Dreiliter mit dem Gabelwinkel von 75 Grad und 48 Ventilen, gibt man 600 PS an, eine charmante Untertreibung. Die Morgengabe des früheren Honda-Motoren-spezialisten Osamu Goto leistet damit offiziell 200 PS weniger als die letzte Generation von ,5-Litern, die vom Gesetzgeber FIA just auf den Schrottplatz der Geschichte entsorgt worden st. Der Wagen ist willig wie ein abgebrühtes Schlachtross, lässt sich selbst aus extremen Driftwinkeln kommod abfangen. Gerhard Bergers Trainingsduell mit Jean Alesi geht 12:5 aus. Aber im Rennen fährt der Franzose stärker, gewinnt in Montreal an seinem 31. Geburtstag mit viel Glück. Nur: Sein erster Sieg für Ferrari wird auch sein letzter sein.

19

The car presented in a relaxed atmosphere on 6 February 1995 was the 412 T2, John Barnard's testimony to simple lines and simple solutions. An output of 600 bhp was claimed for its light and compact V12 power plant, with three litres, 48 valves and cylinder banks at an angle of 75 degrees. That was undoubtedly a charming understatement. Officially, the morning gift of former Honda engine specialist Osamu Goto was 200 bhp less potent than the last-generation 3.5-litre units which had just been thrown on the scrap heap of history by the FIA. The car was as good-natured as a callous war-horse. It could be corrected comfortably even from extreme drift angles. Berger's practice duel with Alesi finished 12:5 in the Austrian's favour. But in the actual races the Frenchman was more aggressive, securing a lucky win at Montreal on his 31st birthday. His first victory for Ferrari would also be his last.

World Championship

1 Michael Schumacher (102)
2 Damon Hill (69)
3 David Coulthard (49)
4 Johnny Herbert (45)
5 Jean Alesi (42)
6 Gerhard Berger (31)
7 Mika Hakkinen (17)
8 Olivier Panis (16)
9 Heinz-Harald Frentzen (15)
10 Mark Blundell (13)
11 Rubens Barrichello (11)
12 Eddie Irvine (10)
13 Martin Brundle (7)
14 Gianni Morbidelli (5)
14 Mika Salo (5)
16 Jean-Christophe Boullion (3)
17 Aguri Suzuki (1)
17 Pedro Lamy (1)

São Paulo (BR), Jean Alesi

Silverstone (GB), Gerhard Berger

Monaco, start crash

Monaco

Montreal (CDN), Jean Alesi, winner

Hockenheim (D), Gerhard Berger giving Hakkinen a lift

Nürburgring (EU), Gerhard Berger

Monza (I), Jean Alesi

1995

Estoril (P), Gerhard Berger

Bestürzt wegen der anhaltenden Titel-Dürre, ringt sich Fiat-Chef Gianni Agnelli zur Rosskur durch. Er verschreibt dem lahmenden Hengst von Maranello das Medikament Michael Schumacher, das beste auf dem Markt und das teuerste. Es wirkt sofort. Unter dem Deutschen fährt Barnards vierschrötiger F310 Siege in Barcelona, Spa und Monza ein. Sein Name kündet vom Mord an einer heiligen Kuh: Im Nacken der Piloten Schumacher und Eddie Irvine kreischt ein Zehnzylinder. In den Champagner des Erfolgs träufelt indessen auch Wermut. So feuert der V10 den Starpiloten des Scuderia in Magny-Cours zwar auf Startplatz eins, verreckt aber in der Einführungsrunde. Und in Montreal trennt sich eine Antriebswelle vom Rest des Wagens. Ende der Saison rücken Ross Brawn als technischer Direktor und Rory Byrne als Chefdesigner von Benetton nach. Die Zukunft sieht rosig aus.

Deeply worried by the lasting title drought, Fiat supremo Gianni Agnelli decided on a kill-or-cure remedy. The medicine prescribed for the lame Maranello stallion was Michael Schumacher, the best and most expensive on the market. It worked at once. With the German at the wheel, John Barnard's chunky F310 notched up wins at Barcelona, Spa and Monza. Its name indicated that a sacred cow had been slaughtered: It was a ten-cylinder unit that whined in the engine bay behind Schumacher and his lieutenant Eddie Irvine. But victory was tempered by the car's precarious reliability. The pole winner of the Scuderia's star driver suffered an engine failure on the parade lap in Magny-Cours, while his left driveshaft parted company with the rest in Montreal. At the end of the season, Ross Brawn and Rory Byrne were lured over from Benetton as technical director and chief designer respectively. The future looked bright.

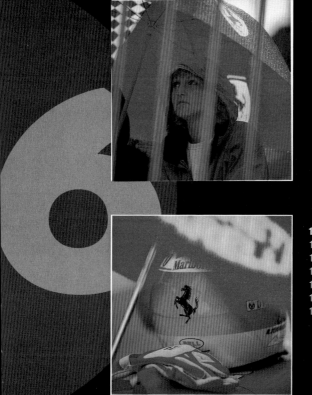

World Championship

1 Damon Hill (97)
2 Jacques Villeneuve (78)
3 Michael Schumacher (59)
4 Jean Alesi (47)
5 Mika Hakkinen (31)
6 Gerhard Berger (21)
7 David Coulthard (18)
8 Rubens Barrichello (14)
9 Olivier Panis (13)
10 Eddie Irvine (11)
11 Martin Brundle (8)
12 Heinz Harald Frentzen (7)
13 Mika Salo (5)
14 Johnny Herbert (4)
15 Pedro Diniz (2)
16 Jos Verstappen (1)

Melbourne (AUS), Michael Schumacher

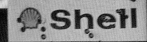

1

GOODYEAR

MAGNETI
MARELLI

GE

Estoril (P)

Magny-Cours (F), Michael Schumacher and Ignazio Lunetta

Imola (RSM), Michael Schumacher

Hockenheim (D), Michael Schumacher

Barcelona (E), Michael Schumacher, Jean Todt

Barcelona (E), Michael Schumacher passing Villeneuve

Barcelona (E), Michael Schumacher, 1st win for Ferrari

Barcelona (E), Michael Schumacher, Jean Todt, podium

GRAN PREMIO MARLBORO DE ESPAÑA 1996

1996

Barcelona (E), Michael Schumacher

Der F310B ist Abschiedspräsent und Erblast zugleich, hinterlassen von John Barnard. Der Brite hat den Dienst für die Scuderia bereits vor der Saison quittiert. Ein paar Eingriffe durch Rory Byrne bleiben Kosmetik. Ebenfalls der Vergangenheit gehört das klassische Ferrarirot an. Der Wagen leuchtet nun in der Feuerfarbe des Sponsors Marlboro. Mit den vier Siegen von Monaco, Montreal, Magny-Cours und Spa bis zum Gran Premio d'Italia erobert sich Michael Schumacher die vorläufige Führung im Championat. In den letzten fünf Läufen jedoch sammelt er, erneut sekundiert von Eddie Irvine, nur noch zwölf weitere Punkte, inklusive einem weiteren ersten Platz in Suzuka. Zum Finale in Jerez reist man mit zartem Optimismus und einem Zähler Vorsprung vor Jacques Villeneuve im Williams. Der übersteht nur leicht lädiert einen unklugen Rammstoß des Deutschen und der Frankokanadier ist Champion.

The F310B, gently updated by Rory Byrne, was both a parting present and a liability, bequeathed by John Barnard, who had left the Scuderia before the season even began. The traditional Ferrari red was also a thing of the past, the car now painted in the fiery colour of sponsor Marlboro. Four victories up to the Italian Grand Prix, in Monaco, Montreal, Magny-Cours and Spa, gave Schumacher an early lead in the title chase. Again loyally assisted by Eddie Irvine, he was able to score just another twelve points in the last five outings, a win in Suzuka included. For the finale at Jerez, Ferrari arrived cautiously optimistic, with a one-point lead over Jacques Villeneuve. The Franco-Canadian's Williams survived a desperate last-ditch lunge by the German, slightly dented, and Villeneuve was champion. The incident resulted in Schumacher's disqualification from second place in the table.

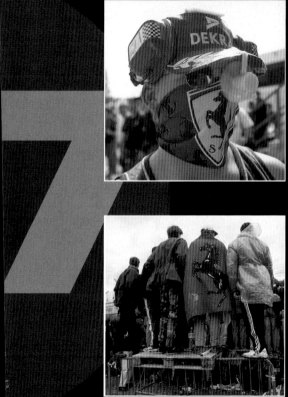

Imola (RSM), Eddie Irvine

Barcelona (E), Eddie Irvine

Barcelona (E), Eddie Irvine

1997

Barcelona (E)

Monaco, Michael Schumacher, winner

Nürburgring (L), Eddie Irvine

A1-Ring (A), Eddie Irvine colliding with Jean Alesi

A1-Ring (A), Eddie Irvine

Hockenheim (D), Michael Schumacher, 2nd, with Fisichella as passenger

Hungaroring (H)

Hungaroring (H), Michael Schumacher

Jerez (EU), Michael Schumacher, Jacques Villeneuve

Jerez (EU), Michael Schumacher

Der Formel-1-Ferrari opus 44 seit 1950 ist wieder unverfälschte Hausmacherkost: Er wird ausschließlich in Maranello entworfen und gebaut. Die Bänke des V10 spreizen sich im Winkel von 80 Grad gegenüber 75 Grad beim Vorgänger. Das senkt den Schwerpunkt ab. Durch die Verwendung kostbarer Werkstoffe verkraftet das Triebwerk höhere Temperaturen und ist leichter geworden wie auch das kompakte Getriebe, das zum erstenmal seit 1992 wieder längs eingebaut ist. Soviel Novität und Innovation verdient einen neuen Namen: F300. Nach uraltem Brauch des Hauses steht die Zahl für das Volumen eines Zylinders. Allerdings vermag man den Vorzug der kurzen Wege noch nicht in den ersehnten Erfolg umzumünzen. Zwar siegt Schumacher sechsmal und bewahrt sich bis zum Finale in Suzuka eine Chance. Dort verspielt er Pole und Championat, als beim Vorstart der Motor abstirbt.

The Formula 1 Ferrari opus 44 since 1950 was again an unalloyed in-house product. It was designed and built exclusively in Maranello. The V10's cylinder banks were angled at 80 degrees, unlike its predecessors' 75, allowing the centre of gravity to be lowered. The power train was made of expensive state-of-the-art materials, permitting lower weight and higher running temperatures. The light and compact gearbox was mounted longitudinally for the first time since 1992. Almost everything was new, and so the Scuderia gave the car a new name: the F300. Following time-honoured tradition at Maranello, the figure stood for the volume of a single cylinder. But all the same, the policy of shortcuts did not lead to the long longed-for success. Schumacher did win six times and headed into the Japanese Grand Prix with a chance of the title. But he threw it away by stalling on the parade lap from pole.

World Championship

1 Mika Hakkinen (100)
2 Michael Schumacher (86)
3 David Coulthard (56)
4 Eddie Irvine (47)
5 Jacques Villeneuve (21)
6 Damon Hill (20)
7 Heinz Harald Frentzen (17)
7 Alexander Wurz (17)
9 Giancarlo Fisichella (16)
10 Ralf Schumacher (14)
11 Jean Alesi (9)
12 Rubens Barrichello (4)
13 Mika Salo (3)
13 Pedro Diniz (3)
15 Johnny Herbert (1)
15 Jan Magnussen (1)
15 Jarno Trulli (1)

Imola (RSM), Eddie Irvine

Monaco, Eddie Irvine

1998

Monaco, Michael Schumacher

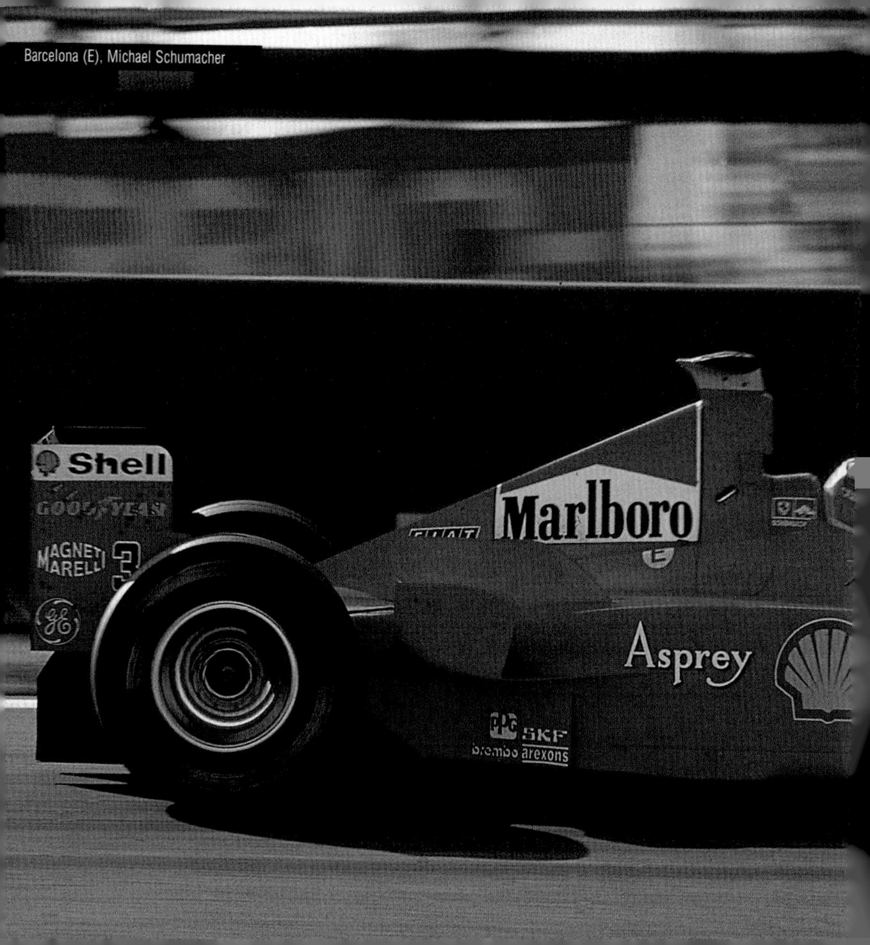

Barcelona (E), Michael Schumacher

Magny-Cours (F): Doppelsieg für Ferrari, nachdem Irvine Schumacher den Rücken freigehalten hat.
Magny-Cours (F): Double victory for Ferrari with Schumacher 1st, Irvine having fended off all threats from behind.

Spa-Francorchamps (B), Eddie Irvine's Ferrari after start crash

Spa-Francorchamps (B), Michael Schumacher into the pits after colliding with David Coulthard

Hungaroring (H), winners' trophies

Hungaroring (H), Michael Schumacher, winner, podium

Former team member

F1/86, Michele Alboreto

Carlo Amadessi, see also Design Monza

500, John Surtees ▲　246, Phil Hill ▼

Monza (I) 600 Grand Prix for Ferrari

312T, René Arnoux ▲　500, J. Surtees ▼

Monza (l) Michele Alboreto, Gerhard Berger, René Arnoux, Phil Hill, John Surtees, Luca Badoer

Beinahe hätte es 1999 geklappt: Der F399 erweist sich als unkompliziert und benutzerfreundlich, leichter zu fahren und einzustellen als der F300. Überdies glänzt er durch kumpelhafte Verlässlichkeit. Dazu trägt vor allem sein V10 bei, rund 15 Kilogramm schwerer und eine Idee größer als sein Pendant bei Mercedes, aber leichter zu installieren, stabiler und insgesamt umgänglicher. Doch dann wird Michael Schumacher durch den Beinbruch von Silverstone für sieben Rennen lahm gelegt mit Mika Salo als Urlaubsvertretung. Eddie Irvine schlägt sich wacker, wächst auch mit seiner Aufgabe mit ersten Plätzen in Melbourne, Spielberg, Hockenheim und Sepang, unterfüttert mit zweiten in Monaco und Silverstone, wird als Titelanwärter aufgebaut. Aber beim Finale in Japan zeigt er unter Druck Wirkung, Zeichen von Resignation, nur Rang drei, Platzen aller Blütenträume.

It looked like plain sailing in 1999. The F399 revealed itself to be uncomplicated and user-friendly, easier to drive and to set up than its predecessor the F300. Moreover, the red car was thoroughly dependable. That was above all due to its V10 engine. It was 15 kilos heavier and slightly bigger than its Mercedes counterpart, but easier to install, more stable and drivable as a whole. Then, however, Michael Schumacher had to stay away from the circuits for seven races as a convalescent because of his Silverstone leg injuries, with Mika Salo as his stand-in. Eddie Irvine did a fine job, growing with his task , scoring victories in Melbourne, Spielberg, Hockenheim and Sepang, supported by seconds in Monaco and Silverstone, even aspiring to the title. But the Ulsterman cracked under pressure in the Suzuka finale, showing symptoms of resignation, third place only and evaporation of all his high-flying dreams.

World Championship

1 Mika Hakkinen (76)
2 Eddie Irvine (74)
3 Heinz Harald Frentzen (54)
4 David Coulthard (48)
5 Michael Schumacher (44)
6 Ralf Schumacher (35)
7 Rubens Barrichello (21)
8 Johnny Herbert (15)
9 Giancarlo Fisichella (13)
10 Mika Salo (10)
11 Jarno Trulli (7)
11 Damon Hill (7)
13 Alexander Wurz (3)
13 Pedro Diniz (3)
15 Olivier Panis (2)
15 Jean Alesi (2)
17 Pedro de la Rosa (1)
17 Marc Gene (1)

Imola (RSM), Michael Schumacher

Imola (RSM), Michael Schumacher, practice

Imola (RSM), Michael Schumacher, Jean Todt

1999

Imola (RSM), Michael Schumacher, winner

Monaco, Michael Schumacher, winner

Magny-Cours (F), Eddie Irvine

Magny-Cours (F), Eddie Irvine

Montreal (CDN), Michael Schumacher

Hockenheim (D), Mika Salo

Hockenheim (D), Eddie Irvine

Sepang (MAL), Michael Schumacher having recovered from his Silverstone accident

1999

Sepang (MAL), Eddie Irvine, winner

Sepang (MAL), Michael Schumacher 2nd

Neuer Name, neues Glück. Der V V 2000 scheint seinem Vorgänger zu gleichen und ist doch ganz anders. Um zehn auf 102 Kilogramm abgemagert, präsentiert sich der V10 frühlingsschlank. Der Gabelwinkel wurde auf 90 Grad erweitert, der Schwerpunkt somit erneut abgesenkt. Zu denkbar kompakten Dimensionen ist die Übertragung geschrumpft, vor allem das Differential. Erstmals bestehen die Schlüsselelemente der Aufhängung aus Karbon. Aber auch geborene Sieger haben Schwächen. In der Hitze des Gefechts entwickelt der F1-2000 einen Heißhunger auf Hinterreifen. Gleichwohl fügen sich die Dinge im Auf und Ab zu Schumachers erstem Ferrari-Titel, drei Anfangserfolge in Melbourne, Sao Paulo und Imola, die beiden zwischendurch am Nürburgring und in Montreal, die vier am Ende in Monza, Indianapolis, Suzuka und Sepang. Götterdämmerung...

20

Sometimes a new name means a new chance. The F1-2000 seemed to resemble its predecessor but was so different. With 102 kilos, the latest variant of the V10 was an impressive ten kilos lighter than the previous year's powerplant. The angle between the cylinder banks had again been widened, to 90 degrees to lower the centre of gravity. The transmission, above all the differential, had shrunk to even more compact dimensions. For the first time the key components of the suspension were made of carbon fibre. But born winners have their weaknesses, too. In the heat of the battle, the F1-2000 tended to devour its rear tyres. Though, despite ups and downs, the season yielded Michael Schumacher's first Ferrari title, three initial wins in Melbourne, Sao Paulo and Imola, two in between at the Nürburgring and in Montreal, his last four in Monza, Indianapolis, Suzuka and Sepang. Twilight of the gods

World Championship

1. **M.Schumacher (108)**
2. Mika Hakkinen (89)
3. David Coulthard (73)
4. **Rubens Barrichello (62)**
5. Ralf Schumacher (24)
6. Giancarlo Fisichella (18)
7. Jacques Villeneuve (17)
8. Jenson Button (12)
9. Heinz Harald Frentzen (11)
10. Jarno Trulli (6)
10. Mika Salo (6)
12. Jos Verstappen (5)
13. Eddie Irvine (4)
14. Ricardo Zonta (3)
15. Alexander Wurz (2)
15. Pedro de la Rosa (2)

Melbourne (AUS), Michael Schumacher, winner

São Paulo (BR), Michael Schumacher, winner

São Paulo (BR), Michael Schumacher

Nürburgring (EU), Michael Schumacher, winner

Montreal (CDN), Schumacher and Barrichello, 1st and 2nd

Magny-Cours (F), Michael Schumacher

Magny-Cours (F), Michael Schumacher's Ferrari

Magny-Cours (F), Michael Schumacher

Spielberg (A), Michael Schumacher after spin

Hockenheim (D), Michael Schumacher, spinning off after the start after colliding with Giancarlo Fisichella

Hockenheim (D), Rubens Barrichello, winner

Hockenheim (D), Rubens Barrichello and Mika Häkkinen

Monza (I), start

Monza (I), Michael Schumacher, winner

Monza (I), Michael Schumacher, winner

Monza (I), podium

Monza (I)

2000

Sepang (MAL), Michael Schumacher, winner

Indianapolis (USA), Michael Schumacher, winner

Suzuka (J), Michael Schumacher, Jean Todt

Sepang (MAL), victorious Ferrari team

Der Bann ist gebrochen. Bereits das Autodromo di Monza betritt Schumacher als alter und neuer Triumphator, obwohl sich dort ein Ehrentreffer für Juan Pablo Montoya im BMW-Williams in die neun Saisonsiege des erstaunlichen Deutschen einlagert. Mit 52 Grand-Prix-Erfolgen ist der längst auf dem Wege zu neuen Ufern. Kein Wunder: Der beste Michael Schumacher aller Zeiten trifft auf den besten Ferrari der Geschichte, den F2001, nach sieben Monaten Entwicklung den Medien und damit der Welt vorgestellt am 29. Januar in Fiorano. Die Nase pfeilt viel tiefer im Fahrtwind als gehabt. Auf 96 Kilo heruntergetrimmt hat man den V10, verbessert überdies hinsichtlich seiner Leistung, seines Stehvermögens, seiner Ausdauer, seiner Umgänglichkeit. Jede einzelne Komponente der Aufhängung wurde überdacht, Ziel: eine perfekte Symbiose mit den Bridgestone-Reifen. Sie klappt.

The spell was broken. As early as Spa, Schumacher presented himself to the crowd as world champion old and new, after notching up his 52nd grand prix victory. In Monza a fortnight later he was applauded like a Roman emperor by the tifosi, although there Juan Pablo Montoya in the BMW-Williams interrupted the German's run of nine wins in 2001. His amazing dominance was no miracle. The best Schumacher of all time was in league with the best Ferrari in history – the F2001. After seven months of development, it was presented to the media and the world at Fiorano on 29 January. The nose was much lower than seen on the 2000 model, the engine six kilos lighter, further improved in terms of its performance, reliability, consumption and driveability. There had been a basic review of all suspension elements to maximise the performance of the Bridgestone tyres. It worked.

World Championship

1 **Michael Schumacher (123)**
2 David Coulthard (65)
3 **Rubens Barrichello (56)**
4 Ralf Schumacher (49)
5 Mika Hakkinen (37)
6 Juan Pablo Montoya (31)
7 J.Villeneuve (12)
7 Nick Heidfeld (12)
7 Jarno Trulli (12)
10 Kimi Raikkonen (9)
11 G.Fisichella (8)
12 Eddie Irvine (6)
12 Heinz-Harald Frentzen (6)
14 Olivier Panis (5)
14 Jean Alesi (5)
16 Pedro de la Rosa (3)
17 Jenson Button (2)
18 Jos Verstappen (1)

Melbourne (AUS), Michael Schumacher, winner

Imola (RSM), Michael Schumacher

Barcelona (E), Michael Schumacher, pole position

Monaco, Michael Schumacher

Monaco, Michael Schumacher, winner

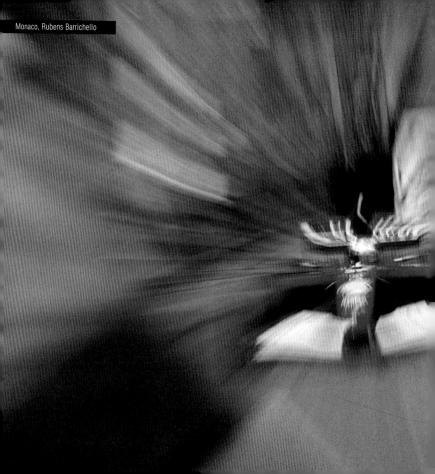
Monaco, Rubens Barrichello

Monaco, Michael Schumacher, winner

Nürburgring (EU), Michael Schumacher, winner

Silverstone (GB), Michael Schumacher in Gonzalez' 1951 Ferrari Tipo 375

Magny-Cours (F), Michael Schumacher, winner

Magny-Cours (F), Michael Schumacher

Hungaroring (H), Michael Schumacher 1st, Rubens Barrichello 2nd, Schuey already 2001 champion

Hungaroring (H), Schumacher, Todt, Barrichello

Spa-Francorchamps (B)

Spa-Francorchamps (B), start

Spa-Francorchamps (B), Michael Schumacher

Monza (I), Michael Schumacher

Suzuka (J), Michael Schumacher, winner

Suzuka (J), Stefano Domenicali, team manager

immer kürzere Intervalle, immer totalere Triumphe. Schon in Magny-Cours ist Schumacher Fünffach-Champion, so dass sich die Scuderia anschickt, seinen Kollegen Rubens Barrichello auf Platz zwei in der Endwertung zu hieven. Bereits in Budapest hat man den Titel bei den Konstrukteuren eingesackt. In Melbourne und Sepang muss noch der glorreiche Gebrauchtwagen F2001 herhalten. In Interlagos verfügt der Deutsche, in Imola auch der Brasilianer über die "rote Göttin" F2002. Das perfekte Auto? So scheint es: Gefällige Linien, in welche die aero-dynamisch ausgeklügelten Aufhängungen eingebunden sind, und ein fein skulptiertes Heck umkleiden vielfältigen Fortschritt, zeugen selbst davon. Panharmonie und Synergie sind das Gebot der Stunde, die geschmeidige Kooperation auch mit Partnern wie Bridgestone und Shell. Für die Zukunft sieht die Branche Rot.

20

Ever shorter became the intervals, ever more total the triumphs. As early as Magny-Cours, Schumacher had his fifth title under his belt. The Scuderia could set about manoeuvring is team mate since 2000, Rubens Barrichello, into second place in the final standings. As early as Budapest, Ferrari secured the constructors' championship for the fourth consecutive ime. For Melbourne and Sepang, the glorious F2001 was lured out of retirement. At Interlagos, he "Red Goddess" F2002 was only at the disposal of the German, at Imola for both drivers. he car seemed to verge on perfection. Sleek lines that also comprehended its aerodynamically ophisticated suspension, and a finely sculpted rear end clothed an abundance of progress, s well as being part and parcel of it. Panharmony and synergy were of prime necessity, even ith outward partners like Bridgestone and Shell. The future looked red.

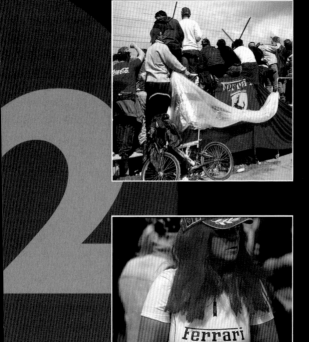

World Championship

1 **Michael Schumacher (144)**
2 **Rubens Barrichello (77)**
3 Juan Pablo Montoya (50)
4 Ralf Schumacher (42)
5 David Coulthard (41)
6 Kimi Raikkonen (24)
7 Jenson Button (14)
8 Jarno Trulli (9)
9 Eddie Irvine (8)
10 Nick Heidfeld (7)
10 Giancarlo Fisichella (7)
12 Jacques Villeneuve (4)
12 Felipe Massa (4)
14 Olivier Panis (3)
15 Mark Webber (2)
15 Takuma Sato (2)
15 Mika Salo (2)
15 Heinz-Harald Frentzen (2)

Imola (RSM), Rubens Barrichello

Imola (RSM)

Imola (RSM), Michael Schumacher, winner

Imola (RSM), Michael Schumacher, Rubens Barriche

Imola (RSM), Michael Schumacher, immediately after the start

A1-Ring (A), start

A1-Ring (A), Rubens Barrichello letting Schumacher pass for victory

A1-Ring (A), Michael Schumacher, Rubens Barrichello

Monaco, Michael Schumacher

Montreal (CDN), Michael Schumacher, winner

2002

Nürburgring (EU), Rubens Barrichello, winner

Magny-Cours (F), Michael Schumacher during qualifying

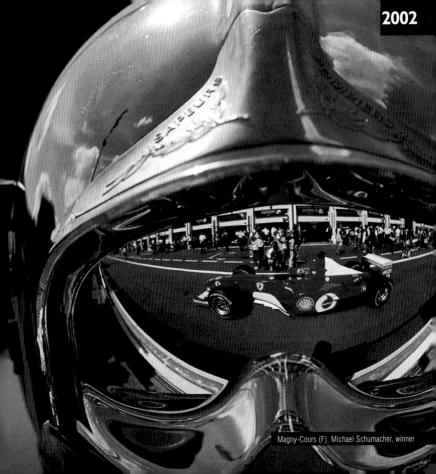

Magny-Cours (F), Michael Schumacher, winner

Magny-Cours (F): Alle für einen. Der Triumph ist auch eine Leistung des Teams.

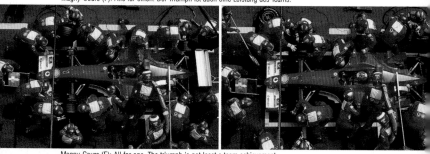

Magny-Cours (F): All for one. The triumph is not least a team achievement.

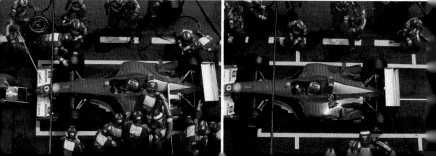

2002

Magny-Cours (F), Michael Schumacher

Magny-Cours (F), Michael Schumacher

Magny-Cours (

Magny-Cours (F), Michael Schumacher, winner

Magny-Cours (F), Michael Schuma

Magny-Cours (F): Weltmeisterschaft Nummer 5 für Schumacher in Rekordzeit. Sieben Rennen stehen noch aus.
Magny-Cours (F): Schumacher's fifth title being achieved in record time, with seven races to go.

Hockenheim (D), Michael Schumacher, winner

2002

Monza (I), Michael Schumacher 2nd, Rubens Barrichello 1st

Monza (I), podium

Indianapolis (USA)

Indianapolis (USA), Michael Schumacher, Rubens Barrichello

Hungaroring (H), Michael Schumacher, Jean Todt, Rubens Barrichello, winner

ür den Großen Preis von Deutschland 1956 wurde als Motto ausgegeben: "Jugend stürmt gegen Fangio". Sie tut's vergebens – dieser 45-jährige hat sie noch immer alle fest im Griff. "Jugend stürmt gegen Schumacher" könnte über der Saison 2003 stehen. So manches kommt den Youngstern dabei zugute. Die FIA hat Ferrari-feindliche Gesetze erlassen: Einzelzeitfahren zur Ermittlung der Startplätze, anschließend Tabu für die Autos bis zum Rennen. Die Bridgestone-Walzen der Scuderia ziehen häufig den Kürzeren gegenüber den Michelin-Pneus der Konkurrenz. Und der aktuelle F2003-GA ist den anderen nicht jenen Quantensprung voraus wie sein Vorgänger. Vor Indy machen sich auch noch Juan Pablo Montoya (BMW-Williams) und Kimi Raikkönen (McLaren Mercedes) Hoffnungen, vor Suzuka nur noch der Finne. Den Titel, seinen sechsten, holt Schumacher, bei den Marken Ferrari – zum fünften Mal hintereinander...

20

The motto for the German Grand Prix in 1956 was "The young storm against Fangio". They did so in vain – that 45-year-old was still nonpareil. "The young storm against Schumacher" could have been written across the 2003 season. Conditions were propitious. The new FIA format was very much anti-Ferrari, decreeing one-shot qualification runs and the cars taboo between qualification and race. The Scuderia's Bridgestone tyres were frequently outshone by the Michelin rubber of its competitors. And the latest F2003-GA was not that far ahead, compared to its predecessor. Before Indy, two more drivers still had their eyes firmly set upon the title, Juan Pablo Montoya (BMW-Williams) and Kimi Raikkonen (McLaren Mercedes), before Suzuka only the Finn had a slim chance. But the championship, his sixth, was secured by Michael Schumacher, the constructors' by Ferrari – for the fifth consecutive time.

World Championship

Monaco, Michael Schumacher

Monaco, Rubens Barrichello

A1-Ring (A), Michael Schumacher, winner

A1-Ring (A), Michael Schumacher

Monza (I), Michael Schumacher

2003

Indianapolis (USA), Michael Schumacher, winner

Indianapolis (USA), Schumacher, Paolo Martinelli

Indianapolis (USA), Michael Schumacher

Indianapolis (USA), Michael Schumacher

Suzuka (J), Michael Schumacher

2003

Suzuka (J), Rubens Barrichello, winner

Suzuka (J), pitstop Michael Schumacher

Suzuka (J), podium

Suzuka (J), Jean Todt and Michael Schumacher

Suzuka (J), team-photo, worldchampionchip

Die Vorgänge unterhalb des riesigen diskförmigen Rostrums bei der Siegerehrung in Monza 2003 zeigten es wieder einmal deutlich: Andere mögen Respekt, alle Achtung oder gar Staunen erzeugen. Das Phänomen Ferrari aber löst Leidenschaft pur aus. Dabei haben Bernie Ecclestones kraftvolle Preispolitik und die erschlaffende Wirkung des heimischen Fernsehsessels die rasenden und eifernden tifosi von einst längst zum gepflegten Konzertpublikum weichgespült. Noch immer lässt der älteste Rennstall im Geschäft die Seelen überkochen wie kein zweiter. Und selbst zu den Zeiten unsäglicher Krisen galt es als das höchste Glück des Rennfahrers, für die Scuderia zu starten. Doch Vorsicht: Die Piloten standen vor allem immer im Dienst des enigmatischen Alten Enzo Ferrari und des Imperiums, waren allenfalls Hohepriester und nie die Götter selbst. Sogar ein Michael Schumacher ist da nur ein besonders brillanter Offizier, ein Rubens Barrichello ein ungewöhnlich sympathischer und linientreuer Adjutant. Der ehrfürchtige Kosename "rote Göttin" für den F2002 beweist es: Die Autos sind die Idole, der Rest ist Religion.

The delirium in red beneath the huge disc-shaped rostrum during this year's winners' celebration in Monza left no doubt at all: Others may cause respect, awe or even amazement. The Ferrari phenomenon, however, triggers pure passion, although Bernie Ecclestone's vigorous pricing policy and the slackening effect of their TV armchairs have softened the once raving and screaming tifosi into a refined concert audience. The oldest racing stable in the business is still second to none when it comes to making people's souls boil over. And even during periods of crisis that defied description it was considered as a racing driver's greatest happiness to be a member of the Scuderia. But things are not that simple: the drivers have always been employees of the enigma that was Enzo Ferrari or of the Ferrari empire, high priests rather than the gods themselves. Even Michael Schumacher is, above all, a brilliant officer, Rubens Barichello an unusually personable and loyal aide-de-camp. The reverential sobriquet for the F2002 shows it clearly: It is the cars that are the idols. The rest is religion.

Alberto Ascari, Bern (CH)

Der Mailänder Bürger Ascari, seines Zeichens Fiat-Händler, verheiratet mit einer netten Frau, Mietta, zwei nette Kinder, Tonio und Patrizia: von einnehmendem Wesen, bescheiden, gesetzesfromm, ein bisschen abergläubisch. Der Rennfahrer Ascari, Champion auf Ferrari 1952 und '53: erdrückend, fast schon demütigend überlegen. Er fährt präzise, besonnen und kalt: Als er in der 81. Runde des Grand Prix de Monaco 1955 an der Schikane in den Hafen fliegt, ist er schon fertig zum Absitzen, während sich sein Wagen zügig dem Mittelmeer nähert. Diesmal kommt er mit einem Nasenbruch und einer Gehirnerschütterung davon. Vier Tage später, am 26. Mai jenes Jahres, erfährt die Welt bestürzt vom Ableben Ascaris, beim privaten Training in Monza mit einem Ferrari-Rennsportwagen, mal eben ein paar Runden, damit er nicht aus der Übung kommt. Niemand hat den Unfall gesehen.

Alberto Ascari (1918-1955)

The Milan citizen Ascari, a Fiat agent by profession, was married to a lovely wife, Mietta, with two lovely children, Tonio and Patrizia. He was personable, modest, law-abiding and a little superstitious. But at the wheel of his Ferrari, Ascari the racing driver, double champion in 1952 and '53, was overwhelmingly, almost humiliatingly superior. He was precise, level-headed and cold. On lap 81 of the 1955 Monaco Grand Prix he flew into the harbour at the notorious chicane. While his car was quickly approaching the Mediterranean, Ascari was already preparing to bale out. He got away with a broken nose and concussion. But four days later, on 26 May, a dumbfounded world was informed that Ascari had met his death, driving a Ferrari sports car at Monza, just for a couple of laps in order to keep his hand in. There were no witnesses.

Nino Farina, Bern (CH)

Piero Taruffi

igi Villoresi, 1953

Alberto Ascari, Bern (CH) 1953

José Froilan Gonzalez, Spa-Francorchamps (B)

Mike Hawthorn, Spa-Francorchamps (B) 1953

Monza (I) 1953, Ferrari drivers Farina, Ascari, Hawthorn, Villor

Sebring 1957, Ferrari team drivers von Trips, Trintignant, Musso, Colli

Am 24. Juni 1911 wird Fangio als eines von sechs Kindern der Eheleute Herminia und Don Loreto Fangio in Balcarce am Atlantik 400 Kilometer südlich von Buenos Aires geboren. In Balcarce wird er am 17. Juli 1995 zur bleibenden Ruhe gebettet, beweint von seiner großen Familie, betrauert von seiner Nation, respektvoll beklagt von der ganzen Welt. Er sei, sagen viele noch viel später, auf ewig der Größte in diesem Sport. In der Dekade zwischen 1950 und 1958 hat sich Fangio in der Tat ein Denkmal gezimmert aus lauter Einmaligkeiten. Mit 24 Siegen in 51 Großen Preisen erzielt er eine Trefferquote von fast 50 Prozent. Bei 48 von ihnen startet er aus der ersten Reihe. Seine fünf Titel, 1951 auf Alfa Romeo, 1954 und 55 auf Mercedes, 1956 auf Ferrari und 1957 auf Maserati, sind dauerhaft verkittet durch den Nimbus der Unbesiegbarkeit und das Mysterium, das man Persönlichkeit nennt.

Juan Manuel Fangio (1911-1995)

Fangio was born at Balcarce on the Atlantic, 400 kilometres south of Buenos Aires, on 24 June 1911, one of six children of Herminia and Don Loreto Fangio. It was at Balcarce again that he was buried on 17 July 1995, bewailed by his large family, lamented by his nation, respectfully mourned by the whole world. He was, and would be, the greatest ever in his sport, said many, even many years later. Indeed, between 1950 and 1958, Fangio had erected his own monument from unique achievements. With 24 victories out of 51 grands prix, his lucky strikes amounted to almost 50 percent. In 48 of them, he started from the first row. His five titles, in 1951 for Alfa Romeo, in 1954 and '55 for Mercedes, in 1956 in a Ferrari and in 1957 in a Maserati, were lastingly welded together by the aura of his invincibility and the inscrutable mystery of what is called personality. His legend endures.

Juan Manuel Fangio, Peter Collins, Nürburgring (D)

1956

Mit Jochen Rindt teilt Mike Hawthorn eine düstere Gemeinsamkeit: Beiden ist nicht mehr vergönnt, als Weltmeister auch nur noch einen Grand Prix zu fahren. Bei Hawthorn hätten sich Talent und Unbeständigkeit miteinander verschränkt, eiskalter Wagemut mit tollen Reflexen, sagt Enzo Ferrari in seiner Autobiographie Piloti, che gente. So wirkt er im Wagen, mehr Passagier als Pilot, ein ewig Gefährdeter. Sein Championat von 1958 fällt knapp aus mit einem Punkt Vorsprung vor dem glücklosen Stirling Moss im Vanwall. Dann erklärt Hawthorn seinen Rücktritt vom Rennsport, zutiefst erschüttert, weil die vergangene mörderische Saison das Leben seiner Kameraden Peter Collins, Luigi Musso und Stuart Lewis-Evans gefordert hat. Am 22. Januar 1959 stirbt er selbst bei einem kleinen Duell auf der Landstraße bei Guildford, eine Frage der Ehre. Irgendwie gleicht sein Sterben seinem Leben.

Mike Hawthorn (1929-1959)

Mike Hawthorn had something gloomy in common with Jochen Rindt: Neither was granted the chance to drive another grand prix after winning the title. Hawthorn was "a disconcerting racer, with his combination of talent and inconsistency, icy and calculated daring and outstanding reflexes," wrote Enzo Ferrari in his autobiography Piloti, che gente. That was the impression he gave at the wheel, a passenger rather than a pilot, forever in jeopardy. His 1958 title was a lucky one, a single point ahead of the luckless Stirling Moss in the Vanwall. Then Hawthorn retired, deeply moved because the murderous season had claimed the lives of his comrades Peter Collins, Luigi Musso and Stewart Lewis-Evans. On 22 January 1959 he was killed himself, as the result of a little duel on the Guildford bypass, for the sake of honour. Somehow his dying resembled the way he had lived.

Mike Hawthorn, Peter Collins

Wolfgang Graf Berghe von Trips, Monza (I) 1957

Die Fahrerweltmeisterschaft ist 95 Grand Prix alt, als man 1961 in Zandvoort dem ersten Deutschen den Lorbeer um die Schultern legt, Wolfgang Graf Berghe von Trips. Das rankt sich um den jungen Adligen bereits ein Mythos, fast schon ein Märchen. Es handelt vom Ritter, der sich ins 20. Jahrhundert und an das Lenkrad eines Rennwagens verirrt hat. Wo Rauch ist, ist auch Feuer. Der Mann hat wirklich sowas, wohnt sogar auf einem richtigen Wasserschloss im Rheinischen, übrigens in derselben Großgemeinde, aus der Michael Schumacher stammt. Seit 1957 startet er für Ferrari und schickt sich nun an, sich die Krone des Weltmeisters aufzusetzen. Neben guten Platzierungen trumpft Trips noch einmal auf mit einem Sieg in Aintree. In Monza kann sich schon alles entscheiden im Duell mit seinem Ferrari-Kollegen Phil Hill. Doch in Runde zwei interveniert der Renntod. Eine Nation trauert.

Wolfgang Graf Berghe von Trips

(1928-1961)

The drivers' world championship was 95 grands prix old when the first German gained his laurels at Zandvoort in 1961, Wolfgang Count Berghe von Trips. At that moment, the young aristocrat was already wrapped in a myth, or rather a fairy tale. It dealt with a knight who had somehow found his way into the twentieth century and the cockpit of a racing car. Where there is smoke, there is also fire. The man had a touch of genuine nobility about him, to the point of living in a real moated castle in the Rhineland, amazingly in the same municipality from where Michael Schumacher comes. Since 1957 he had been a Ferrari driver and was on the verge of notching up the title. He had gathered some more useful points and gained another victory in Aintree. Winning in Monza would decide the count's duel with team mate Phil Hill in his favour. But then Death interfered on lap two. A whole nation mourned.

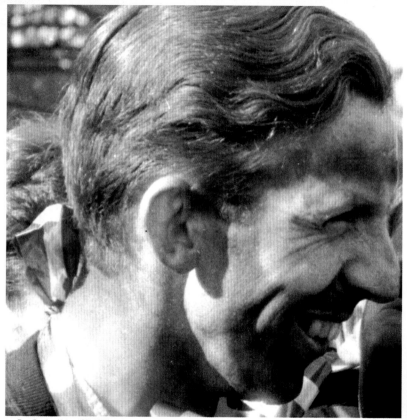
Tony Brooks, Aintree (GB) 1957

1957

Mike Hawthorn

Wolfgang Graf Berghe von Trips

Phil Hill

Enzo Ferrari bescheinigt ihm, bei Langstreckenrennen könne er "seine natürlichen Gaben ausspielen", sein "Gespür für Tempo und Respekt für die Maschine."

Der ideale Schauplatz, mit solchen Talenten zu punkten, ist Le Mans: Dreimal gewinnt Phil Hill das Marathon auf dem Sarthekurs, 1958, 61 und 62. Das ist viel. Die drei Siege insgesamt, mit denen der erste amerikanische Weltmeister in die Annalen des Grand-Prix-Sports eingeht, sind hingegen wenig – gemessen an Standards, die später gesetzt werden. Im Jahre seines Championats 1961 genügen ihm die beiden Erfolge in Spa und Monza. Zwei Dinge spielen ihm dabei in die Karten: Die Dominanz der schlanken Ferrari Tipo 156 und der Tod seines Teamgefährten, des deutschen Reichsgrafen Wolfgang Graf Berghe von Trips in Monza. Von da an geht's bergab in der Formel 1 und 1966 wirft Hill das Handtuch.

Phil Hill (*1927)

Enzo Ferrari used to say that in long distance races Phil Hill "could combine his innate gifts for speed and respect for the machine – a winning combination." The ideal venue for a racing driver to demonstrate such talents is and has always been Le Mans. Hill won the Sarthe marathon three times, in 1958, '61 and '62. That was a lot. But with just three victories, through which the first American world champion went down in history, his grand prix career was less impressive, in particular measured against later standards. His two wins in Spa and Monza sufficed for him to secure his championship in 1961. Two things were in his favour, on the one hand that year's dominance of the slender Ferrari Tipo 156 with its characteristic shark nose, on the other the death of his team mate and rival Count Wolfgang von Trips in Monza. From then onwards, it was downhill in Formula 1, and in 1966 Philip Toll Hill threw in the towel.

Phil Hill, Nürburgring (D)

Ricardo Rodriguez, Nürburgring (D) 1962

Lorenzo Bandini, Nürburgring (D) 19

Willy Mairesse, Spa-Francorchamps (B) 1962

Giancarlo Baghetti, Nürburgring (D)

Willy Mairesse, Spa-Francorchamps (B)

Zugegeben: Sein Titel 1964 für Ferrari hängt am seidenen Faden, wird auf den letzten Drücker in den letzten drei Minuten der Saison beim Finale in Mexiko entschieden. Aber die Sache geht schon in Ordnung. Denn immer, wenn es darauf ankommt, ist Big John wirklich Weltklasse, auch fürs Extremste sensibilisiert durch 68 erste Plätze auf dem Motorrad und die sieben Zweirad-Championate, die seiner Übersiedelung in den Rennwagen 1960 vorausgehen. Am Nürburgring ist das so und in Spa, wenn es Bindfäden regnet – wie 1966. Da siegt John Surtees mit der Sicherheit eines Traumwandlers – und verlässt anschließend Ferrari, mitten in der Saison, Personalquerelen. Von da an sind ihm nur noch zwei Grand-Prix-Siege beschieden, im Cooper und im Honda. An seinen Versuch, zwischen 1970 und 78 mit einem eigenen Rennstall Lorbeer zu erwerben, denkt er heute nur noch mit Verdruss zurück.

John Surtees (*1934)

Admittedly, his title for Ferrari was touch and go, decided at the finale in Mexico City in the dying minutes of the 1964 season. But without any doubt, Big John deserved it. Whenever it really counted, he was world class, fine-honed for Formula 1 by the 68 motor bike wins and the seven championships on two wheels that preceded his change to four wheels in 1960. That is why he excelled at the Nürburgring and in Spa when it was raining cats and dogs, as it did in 1966. It was amidst the Ardennes downpours that he secured his greatest success, with uncanny sureness – only to leave Ferrari in the middle of the season because he was at odds with some of the staff. From then onwards, he had to content himself with just two more victories, in the Cooper and in the Honda. His memories of his own racing stable between 1970 and '78 are not particularly fond. But the man himself and the Surtees legend are still with us.

Monza (I), John Surtees, Jo Bonnier

DUNLOP

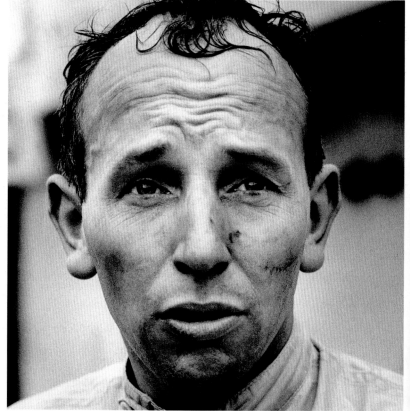

John Surtees, Zandvoort (NL)

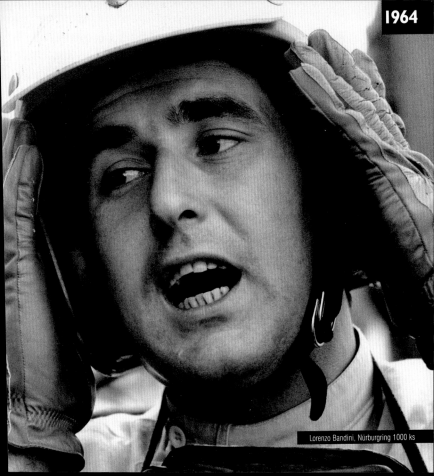

1964

Lorenzo Bandini, Nürburgring 1000 ks

John Surtees, Nürburgring (D)

Lorenzo Bandini, Clermont-Ferrand (F)

1965

STIVA
EFAC-AUTOM
RRARI - MO

Surtees, Clermont-Ferrand (F)

Lorenzo Bandini, Clermont-Ferrand (F)

Lorenzo Bandini, Spa-Francorchamps (B)

John Surtees, Lorenzo Bandini, Spa-Francorchamps (B)

John Surtees, Spa-Francorchamps (B)

Mike Parkes, Spa-Francorchamps (B)

Ludovico Scarfiotti, Zandvoort (NL) 1966

Lorenzo Bandini, Zandvoort (NL) 1966

Chris Amon, Monaco

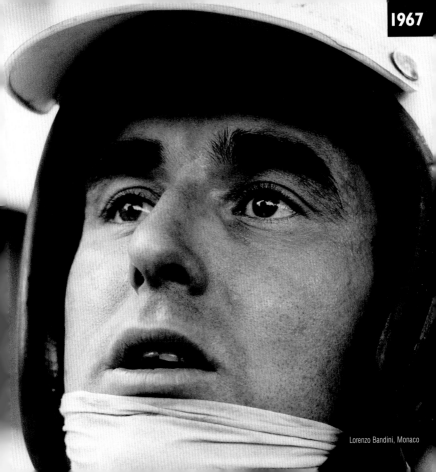

Lorenzo Bandini, Monaco

Chris Amon, Nürburgring (D)

1968

Jacky Ickx, Brands Hatch (GB)

Clay Regazzoni, Monza (I)

Jacky Ickx, Jarama (E)

Clay Regazzoni, Monaco

Mario Andretti, Monza (I) 1972

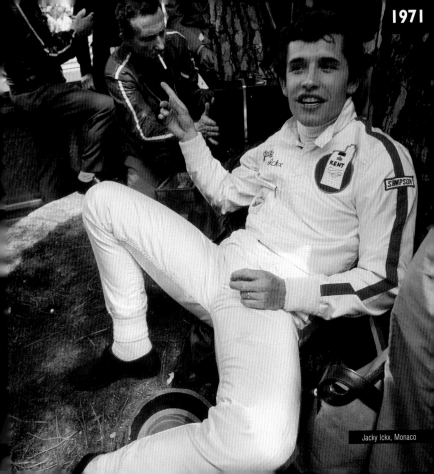

Jacky Ickx, Monaco

Der junge Ickx: ein Draufgänger auf Deubel komm raus. Wie der belgische Bengel 1967 am Nürburgring mit dem winzigen Formel-2-Matra unter den erwachsenen Grand-Prix-Wagen wütet, wird niemand vergessen, der dabei war, Position drei im Training, zeitweiliger Aufenthalt auf Rang vier im Rennen. Der späte Ickx hält sich noch in den Achtzigern am Limit auf, im Sportwagen der Mozart der langen Distanz mit fast 50 Siegen, sechs allein in Le Mans. Er fährt akkurat, als lenke er eine Straßenbahn durch die vorgegebenen Schienen. Die Konstante dazwischen: Charisma, Talent in Massen, das Feingefühl eines Seiltänzers bei Regen wie 1968 in Rouen oder 1971 in Zandvoort. Sechs seiner acht Grand-Prix-Erfolge steuert er zur Bilanz der Scuderia bei in fünf Dienstjahren, ein Hoffnungsträger, der sich manchmal in den Fallstricken der Ferrari-Politik verheddert oder einfach Pech hat.

Jacky Ickx (*1954)

In his storm and stress period, Ickx raced like a man possessed. Nobody who saw it will ever forget the Belgian urchin's progress in the tiny Formula 2 Matra amidst fully-fledged grand prix cars at the Nürburgring in 1967. Third fastest in practice, he carved his way through the field to fourth place during the race. In the eighties Ickx still travelled on the edge, a long-distance Mozart with almost 50 victories to his credit, scoring a record sixth win at Le Mans in 1982. Having sown his wild oats, he drove like clockwork. The constants between those extremes were charisma, loads of natural talent and sublime car control in the wet, as for instance in Rouen in 1968 or in Zandvoort in 1971. In his five years with the Scuderia, he added six of his eight grand prix wins to its total. Jacky Ickx was a luminous figure who sometimes got tangled up in the pitfalls of Ferrari politics or was just haunted by bad luck.

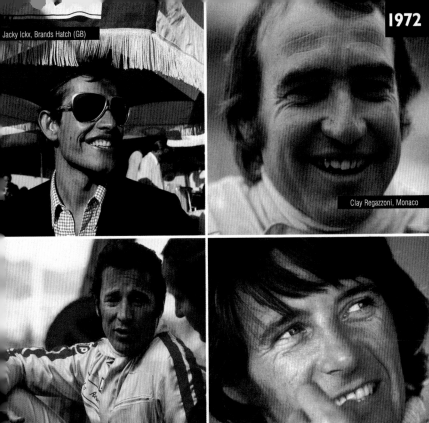

Jacky Ickx, Brands Hatch (GB)

1972

Clay Regazzoni, Monaco

Mario Andretti, Monaco 1971

Firestone

Arturo Merzario, Zeltweg (A) 1973

Clay Regazzoni, Zeltweg (A)

Niki Lauda, Jarama (E)

Manchmal steigt Nikolaus Lauda wieder in die Wagen, die ihn groß machten. Sie wirken quadratisch und grobschlächtig, stampfen und schlingern und driften und sind weit entfernt von der diamantenen Härte und beharrlichen Spurtreue der roten Renner von heute. Einer von ihnen foult ihn am 1. August 1976 im Hinterhof des Nürburgrings für etwas, was wie ein Fahrfehler aussieht, indem er in einem feurigem Inferno sich selbst und fast auch seinen Fahrer zerstört. Sechs Wochen nach seiner Stippvisite in der Hölle sitzt der in Monza erneut im Cockpit und bereits mitten im Mythos, klettert weitere sechs Wochen später im Dauerregen von Fuji vorzeitig aus dem Wagen, verspielt damit wohl Titel Nummer 2 nach 1975. Der stellt sich 1977 ein, ein dritter 1984 im McLaren. Zwischendurch hat Niki Lauda eine schöpferische Pause eingelegt, er wolle nicht mehr im Kreise fahren, sagt er. Karriere mit Synkopen...

Niki Lauda   (*1949)

Sometimes Nikolaus Lauda climbs again into the cars that made him great. They appear square and angular and clumsy, they pitch, toss and drift and are a far cry from the diamond-like firmness and imperturbable tracking stability of today's red racers. One of them fouled him in the backyard of the Nürburgring on 1 August 1976, for something that looked like a driving error, destroying itself and almost its driver in a fiery inferno. Six weeks after his involuntary pitstop in hell, he was back at the wheel at Monza creating a myth, prematurely climbed out of the car in the torrential Fuji rain another six weeks later, thus giving away what might have been his second crown after 1975. He got it in 1977 and a third one in 1984 in a McLaren. In the meantime, Niki Lauda had taken a creative break, fed up, he said, with driving in circles. A syncopated career, and those were only the beginnings.

Niki Lauda, Monaco

Clay Regazzoni, Monaco

Niki Lauda, Montjuich (E)

Niki Lauda, Jarama (E)

Niki Lauda, Long Beach (USA

Niki Lauda, Monaco

Niki Lauda, Nürburgring

Clay Regazzoni, Jarama (E)

Carlos Reutemann, Long Beach (USA)

Niki Lauda, Hockenheim (D)

Gilles Villeneuve, Monaco

Carlos Reutemann, Hockenheim (D)

Gilles Villeneuve, Jody Scheckter, Long Beach (USA)

So richtig aufmerksam auf sich macht er erstmals durch ein Massaker, begangen in Silverstone 1973: Da leistet sich Jody Scheckter am Ende der Startrunde einen Fahrfehler und Sekunden später bedeckt der Schrott von neun Rennwagen die Zielgerade. So richtig verletzt wird niemand. Der wollhaarige Delinquent aus dem südafrikanischen East London hat jedoch seinen Ruf weg als junger Wilder. Es ist sein viertes Rennen für McLaren. „Baby Bear" nennt ihn sein gelassener und unendlich routinierter Mentor und Teamkamerad Denny Hulme. Als ihn nach Jahren bei Tyrrell und Wolf für 1979 der Ruf nach Maranello ereilt, erbringt er selbst eine reife Leistung und kann sich bereits in Monza als Weltmeister feiern lassen. Als ausgewachsener Bär verlässt Scheckter die Scuderia und den Sport Ende der Saison 1980, abgekühlt und leicht verwirrt im emotionalen Abschwung nach seinem Championat.

Jody Scheckter (*1950)

Jody Scheckter jumped into the headlines as a result of his Silverstone massacre, carried out in 1973. At the end of the first lap he made a mistake at Woodcote and seconds later the debris of nine racing cars covered the straight in front of the pits. Nobody was seriously hurt, but the woolly-haired delinquent from South African East London had made a name for himself as a completely fearless daredevil. It was his fourth race for McLaren. His sedate and immensely experienced team-mate and mentor Denny Hulme called him "Baby Bear". When, after years at Tyrrell and Wolf, Scheckter received a call to Ferrari in 1979, he had sown his wild oats and was hailed as new world champion as early as Monza. After the end of the 1980 season, he left the Scuderia as a definitely full-grown bear, mellowed in the ordeal of Formula 1 racing and slightly bewildered in the emotional downswing following his title.

Jody Scheckter, Long Beach (USA)

Mauro Forghieri, Gilles Villeneuve, Jody Scheckter, Hockenheim (D) 1980

Didier Pironi, Mauro Forghieri, Dijoń-Prenois (F)

Über Gilles Villeneuve zu schreiben kommt immer einer Liebeserklärung gleich, an den Mann selber und an diesen Sport. Denn der kleine Frankokanadier, in dessen Gesicht sich Wille und Sensibilität auf faszinierende Weise paaren, verkörpert die Formel 1 wie kein Zweiter. Viele halten ihn für den größten Fahrer aller Zeiten. Er ist immer zu schnell unterwegs, mit dem Snowmobil, mit dem Rennwagen der Formel Atlantic, mit dem Ferrari. Sein Wagemut und seine völlige Furchtlosigkeit kommen zu den Leuten herüber wie Magie, nirgends eindringlicher als in Monza, wo ihn auf seinen Runden ein Aufschrei begleitet. Sie werden austariert durch Villeneuves an Hexerei grenzende Fahrzeugbeherrschung. Aber wie bei den Angehörigen der Artistenfamilie Wallenda bangt man stets, er werde stolpern. Das ereignet sich in Zolder am 8. Mai 1982, letzter Schritt in einem Selbstmord auf Raten.

Gilles Villeneuve (1952-1982)

Writing about Gilles Villeneuve always involves a declaration of love, to the man himself and to the sport his name stands for. That is because the little Franco-Canadian in whose face determination and sensitivity combined in a fascinating way, embodied Formula 1 like nobody else. Many consider him the greatest driver of all time. He would forever drive too fast, with his snowmobile, his Formula Atlantic car, his Ferrari. His daring, aggression and complete fearlessness appealed to the crowd like magic, nowhere more intensely than in Monza, where his laps were accompanied by turmoil among the tifosi. His bravado was counterbalanced by his artistry at the wheel, which bordered on witchcraft. But as with the Flying Wallendas you were always afraid that he might stumble. Stumble he did, in Zolder on 8 May 1982, the last step of a suicide paid in instalments. Enzo Ferrari was disconsolate.

1981

Gilles Villeneuve, Zeltweg (A)

Gilles Villeneuve, Long Beach (USA)

Didier Pironi, Gilles Villeneuve, Long Beach (USA)

René Arnoux, Long Beach (USA)

Alain Prost, Patrick Tambay, Silverstone (GB)

René Arnoux, Imola (RSM)

Michele Alboreto, René Arnoux, Monaco

René Arnoux, Monaco

René Arnoux, Imola (RSM)

1984

Michele Alboreto, Monza (I)

Stefan Johansson, Estoril (P) 1985

1986

ALBORETO

Michele Alboreto, Monaco

Michele Alboreto, Hockenheim (D)

1986

Stefan Johansson, Brands Hatch (GB)

Gerhard Berger, Hockenheim (D) 1987

1988

Michele Alboreto, Monaco

Gerhard Berger, Hockenheim (D)

Michele Alboreto, Monaco

Gerhard Berger, Monaco

Rio de Janeiro (BR), Nigel Mansell, John Barnard

Monaco, Nigel Mansell

Silverstone (GB), Nigel Mansell

Le Castellet (F), Nigel Mansell

Gerhard Berger, Jerez (E)

Nigel Mansell, Estoril (P)

1990

Alain Prost, Estoril (P)

Jean Alesi, Alain Prost, Estoril (P)

Jean Alesi, Estoril (

Jean Alesi, Phoenix (USA)

Bernie Ecclestone, Jean Alesi, Nigel Mansell, Montreal (C

Alain Prost, Hungaroring (H)

Ivan Capelli, Barcelona (E)

1992

Jean Alesi, Imola (RSM)

Jean Alesi, Barcelona (E)

Gerhard Berger, Donington (EU)

Seine gemütliche Schlitzohrigkeit täuscht, mehr noch das dümmliche Klischee vom fidelen Tiroler.Von legerer Lebensart und mit lockeren Sprüchen rasch bei der Hand, ist Gerhard Berger im Cockpit ein entschlossener Mann. Mit 210 Grand Prix zwischen 1984 und 1997, 96 davon in zwei Raten für die Scuderia, gehört er entschieden zu den länger Dienenden in der Branche. Das Glück – oder das Pech – führt ihm Rivalen und Teamkollegen wie Nelson Piquet, Alain Prost, Ayrton Senna, Nigel Mansell oder Michael Schumacher über den Weg. Er misst sich an ihnen mit zehn Siegen, fünf davon für Ferrari. Berger muss auch viel wegstecken, wohl vertraut mit dem Bersten von Rennwagen nach irrwitzigen Abflügen wie 1989 in Imola und 1993 in Monza und Estoril. Den Tod seiner Freunde Senna und Roland Ratzenberger an jenem Schicksalwochenende im Mai 1994 in Imola wird er nie verwinden.

Gerhard Berger (*1959)

His jovial appearance is misleading, even more so the silly cliché of the merry Tyrolean. Certainly Gerhard Berger is cheeky and never at a loss for a cute remark. But in a cockpit he is a determined man. With his 210 grands prix between 1984 and 1997, 96 of which were in the services of the Scuderia, he was among the longest-serving drivers in the sport. He was lucky – or unfortunate – enough to have to pit himself against rivals or team mates like Nelson Piquet, Alain Prost, Ayrton Senna, Nigel Mansell and Michael Schumacher. But he proved his mettle with ten victories, five of them for Ferrari. He also had to put up with the dark side of racing, emerging unscathed from mutilated Ferraris after horrendous crashes in Imola in 1989 or in Monza and Estoril in 1993. But never will he get over the deaths of his friends Senna and Roland Ratzenberger on that disastrous May weekend in 1994.

Zwei Szenen aus dem Leben des Jean Alesi, die erste in Monza am 11. September 1994: Dem Macho-Meeting mit Filmrambo Sylvester Stallone und dem Start aus der Pole Position im Ferrari 412 T1B folgt in Runde 14 der frühe Ausfall, das Getriebe. Da pfeffert Alesi weinend seinen Sturzhelm in seinen privaten Alfa und düst ins heimische Avignon, was das Zeug hält. Die andere Episode und wohl auch der glücklichste Augenblick in seinem Leben bisher: Rückfahrt an die Box huckepack auf Schumachers Benetton in Montreal am 11. Juni 1995. Alesi hat gerade seinen einzigen Grand Prix gewonnen, im Ferrari zumal und auch noch an seinem 31. Geburtstag. Nun heult er hemmungslos in seinen Helm vor lauter Glück. Er ist sizilianischen Geblüts und so wütet Feuer in ihm, zuckt die Nadel seiner Emotionen ständig in den roten Bereich. Eigentlich hat er nie aufgehört, ein Ferrarista zu sein.

Jean Alesi (*1964)

Two scenes from the life of Jean Alesi: The first takes us to Monza, on September 11, 1994. The macho meeting with film-rambo Sylvester Stallone and his start from pole position in the Ferrari 412 T1B were followed by utter frustration as he was forced to retire after 14 laps in the lead because of gearbox trouble. Weeping, he threw his helmet into his private Alfa and raced to the seclusion of his Avignon home. The other episode was arguably the most wonderful moment of his life so far: his return to the pits at Montreal on 11 June 1995, straddling Schumacher's Benetton. He had just won his only grand prix, for Ferrari and on his 31st birthday to boot. So there he was, shedding tears into his helmet because he could not believe his luck. Perhaps it is his Sicilian heritage that has made Alesi such an emotional man. And it is perhaps the reason why he has never stopped being a ferrarista.

Gerhard Berger, Jean Alesi and Jean Todt (left), Hockenheim (D)

1994

Gerhard Berger, Barcelona (E)

Jean Alesi, Estoril (P)

Michael Schumacher, Imola (RSM)

Michael Schumacher, Estoril (P)

Michael Schumacher, Estoril (P)

Michael Schumacher, Magny-Cours (F)

chael Schumacher, Spa-Francorchamps

Eddie Irvine, Buenos Aires (RA)

Eddie Irvine, Magny-Cours (F)

Eddie Irvine, Barcelona (E)

Eddie Irvine, Estoril (P)

1996

Eddie Irvine, São Paulo (BR)

Eddie Irvine, Michael Schumacher, Buenos Aires (RA)

Michael and Ralf Schumacher, Jerez (EU)

Eddie Irvine and his sister Sonja, Monza (I)

Eddie Irvine, Spa-Francorchamps (B)

Michael Schumacher, Nürburgring (L)

502

Eddie Irvine, A1-Ring (A)

Michael Schumacher, A1-Ring (A)

Eddie Irvine, Monza (I)

Michael Schumacher, Montreal (CDN) 1999

1998

Michael Schumacher, Hungaroring (H)

Problemfall Michael Schumacher – nach sechs Titeln und 70 Grand-Prix-Siegen sind dem Mann die noch zu überbietenden Bestleistungen ausgegangen und somit dem Chronisten die Worte. Denn dreizehn Jahre Umgang mit einem solchen Phänomen verschlagen selbst dem Profi die Sprache. Den "Messias vom Kerpener Kreuz" nannten sie ihn einmal ironisch, und in der Tat wurde er zum Gottesgeschenk für das Dream Team aus Maranello. Wie ein rasender Heiland hat er die Karre aus dem Dreck gezogen und den Begriff Ferrari wieder der höchsten Wertschätzung zugeführt, der ihm gebührt. Vielleicht schon zu nachhaltig: Längst macht sich Formel-1-Zar Bernie Ecclestone Sorgen um die TV-Einschaltquoten. Gleichwohl schießt Schumacher-Schrifttum aus dem Boden wie Champignons nach einem milden Sommerregen. Seine Taten sind dokumentiert, kommentiert und analysiert wie die zwölf Arbeiten des Herakles

Michael

Conundrum Michael Schumacher – after six world championships and 70 grand prix victories the man has run out of records to be topped, as his chroniclers have run out of words. Thirteen years of intercourse with a phenomenon like that leave even the professionals speechless. They used to ironically dub him the "Messiah of the Kerpen Cross", alluding to a motorway intersection near his home town, and indeed he turned out to be a godsend to the Maranello dream team. A high-speed saviour, he has straightened out things that lay in a mess when he joined the squad, and elevated the Ferrari name anew to the degrees of appreciation it deserves like nobody else. Perhaps a bit too efficiently: Formula 1 tsar Bernie Ecclestone has long worried about the dwindling audience for his choice spectacle. Nevertheless, Schumacher literature sprouts like mushrooms after a mild summer rain. His deeds have been

in der griechischen Helden-sage. Längst ist er auf dem Weg in Mythos und Legende oder gar schon mitten drin, Figur der Zeitgeschichte und Haushaltsgesicht wie Sir Peter Ustinov, Muhammad Ali oder Pavarotti & Friends. Bereits seine zahlreichen Kose- und Spitznamen zeugen davon: Schumi, Schummy, Schuey oder ganz einfach Schu, da das komplette Wort Schumacher für die Engländer noch immer unaussprechlich ist. Wo die Worte fehlen, nimmt Heldenverehrung gern religiöse Züge an. Während des Grand Prix de Monaco 2000 hing aus dem Appartementblock Shangri-la unmittelbar neben der Rennstrecke ein Bettlaken mit der inbrünstigen Botschaft „Schummy, nur einer ist größer als du!", gefolgt von einer Hand, die geradewegs nach oben in den blauen Himmel über dem Fürstentum zeigte...

Schumacher (*1969)

documented, commented on and analysed like The Twelve Labours of Hercules in the Greek myth. The man himself has long been on his way into myth and legend, or even arrived there, a household name and face like Sir Peter Ustinov, Muhammad Ali or Pavarotti & Friends. His countless pet and nicknames testify to that: Schumi, Schummy, Schuey or simply Schu, because the complete word Schumacher is still a tongue-twister for the average Englishman. When people are at a loss for words, their idolatry tends to adopt religious traits. During the 2000 Monaco Grand Prix, a bed sheet hung out of a window of the luxurious Shangri-La block of flats next to the circuit. It carried the fervent message "Schummy – only one being is greater than you are", flanked by a hand pointing straight to the blue skies above the Principality.

Michael Schumacher, Suzuka (J)

Eddie Irvine, Hungaroring (H)

1999

Mika Salo, Spa-Francorchamps (B)

Eddie Irvine, São Paulo (BR)

Michael Schumacher, Magny-Cours (F)

Michael Schumacher, São Paulo (BR)

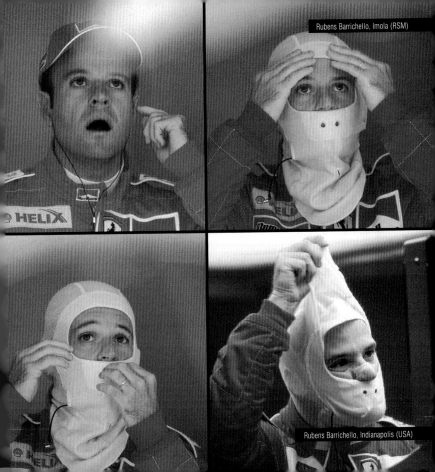

Rubens Barrichello, Imola (RSM)

Rubens Barrichello, Indianapolis (USA)

Die Bilder gehen um die Welt: Rubens Barrichello mit tränennassem Gesicht vor lauter Glück nach seinem ersten Sieg in Hockenheim 2000, Barrichello empört und tief verletzt, nachdem ihn die roten Strategen in Spielberg 2001 per Funk auf Rang drei relegiert haben: Vorfahrt hat Michael Schumacher. Die Amplituden der Leidenschaft sehen bei dem Brasilianer ganz ähnlich aus. Gelegenheit zu beiden Extremen gibt es für ihn genug. Denn in das Glück, für die Scuderia zu fahren, tröpfelt auch Wermut. Zum einen ist da dieser Michael Schumacher, nach allgemeiner Übereinkunft der Größte von allen. Und im Zweifelsfall regiert schnöde die Staatsraison, fallen Entscheidungen grundsätzlich zum höheren Wohl des Hauses Ferrari. Dabei könnte alles so schön sein. Denn auch Rubens Barrichello versteht sich prächtig mit der "roten Göttin" namens F2003 und ihrem Nachfolger F2003-GA, der richtige Mann zur falschen Zeit am richtigen Ort.

Rubens Barrichello (*1972)

The touching pictures could be seen world-wide. They showed Rubens Barrichello, his face drowned in tears, after his first win at Hockenheim in 2000, and outraged and deeply hurt, when the red strategists had relegated him via radio to third in the 2001 Austrian Grand Prix, to the benefit of Michael Schumacher. In the Brazilian's case, the amplitudes of passion look quite similar. These days he is being given generous opportunity to experience both extremes. After all, driving for the Scuderia is a mixed blessing. On the one hand he has to cope with that man Michael Schumacher, universally agreed to be the greatest of them all. On the other, company politics prevail and decisions always have to allow for the welfare of the Ferrari empire as a whole. Alas, things could be so beautiful as Barrichello, too, got along well with the "Red Goddess" F2002 and its successor the F2003-GA, the right man in the right place. Only the time is wrong.

Rubens Barrichello, Hockenheim (D)

Suzuka (J)

Mika Häkkinen, Michael Schumacher, Suzuka (J)

Michael Schumacher, Sepang (MAL)

Häkkinen, Schumacher, Coulthard, Sepang (MAL)

Michael Schumacher, Sepang (MAL)

Michael Schumacher, Rubens Barrichello, Magny-Cours (F)

Rubens Barrichello, Melbourne (AUS)

Michael Schumacher, Indianapolis (USA)

Rubens Barrichello, Indianapolis (USA)

Michael Schumacher, Monza (I)

Michael Schumacher, Melbourne (AUS)

Michael Schumacher, Imola (RSM)

Michael and Ralf Schumacher, Hungaroring (H)

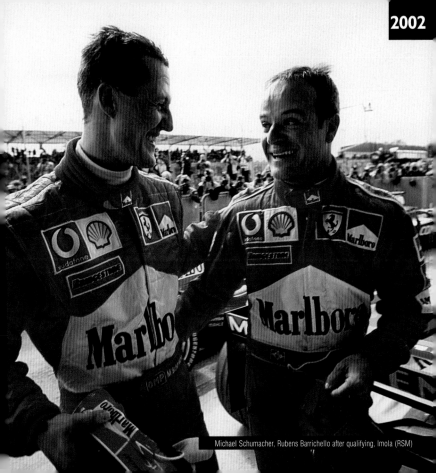

Michael Schumacher, Rubens Barrichello after qualifying, Imola (RSM)

Rubens Barrichello, Michael Schumacher, Indianapolis (USA)

Michael Schumacher, Jean Todt, Monza (I)

Rubens Barrichello, Felipe Massa, São Paulo (BR)

Rubens Barrichello, Monaco

Rubens Barrichello, Monza (I)

hael Schumacher, Magny-Cours (F)

Michael Schumacher, Sepang (MAL)

Froilan Gonzalez' Staubkappe in Monza 1951 hält gerade einmal Dreck, Wind und Fliegen vom rundlichen Haupt des Argentiniers fern. In Michael Schumachers diamanthartem High-Tech-Helm bei der gleichen Gelegenheit 2002 sind Visierheizung, Lüftung und Drehzahlmesser eingearbeitet. Die Evolution des Kopfschutzes bildet den Fortschritt im Rennsport gleichsam noch einmal ab. Schon 1961 trägt etwa der Helm des Grafen Trips das Zeichen der Kölner Scuderia Colonia, schon 1969 krönt das Novum Integralhelm des Sicherheits-Pioniers Jackie Stewart ein Kranz im schottischen Tartanmuster. 1970 wirbt Jochen Rindt mit der Aufschrift "This space to let" auf kahlem Weiß um Werbung: Mit mehr Helm steht auch mehr Fläche dafür zur Disposition, in eigener Sache, für das Anliegen, das Land oder die Marke, die man vertritt, den Sponsor, allerlei graphischen Wirrwarr oder einfach aus Freude am Design. Die Piloten der Scuderia machten da keine Ausnahme.

Froilan Gonzalez' dust cap in Monza 1951 was just suited to keep dirt, wind and flies away from the chubby Argentinian's head. Into Michael Schumacher's diamond-hard high-tech helmet at the same venue in 2002, have been integrated visor heating, a ventilation system as well as the rev counter. The evolution of the drivers' head protection mirrors progress in racing as a whole. As early as 1961, Count von Trips sported the coat of arms of the Cologne Scuderia Colonia on his helmet. In 1968, the integral helmet introduced by the safety-conscious Jackie Stewart was crowned by the Scot's tartan band. In 1970, Jochen Rindt touted for advertising with the inscription "This space to let" on the bare white of his helmet. More space meant more opportunity to further one's own cause, boost one's message, country, team or sponsor, flaunt sundry graphic mess or just beautiful and unusual design. The Scuderia's drivers have been no exception.

Juan Manuel Fangio, Zandvoort (NL)

Willy Mairesse, Spa-Francorchamps (B)

Lorenzo Bandini, Monza (I)

Ricardo Rodriguez, 1000 Kms Nürburgring (D)

Phil Hill, Monza (I)

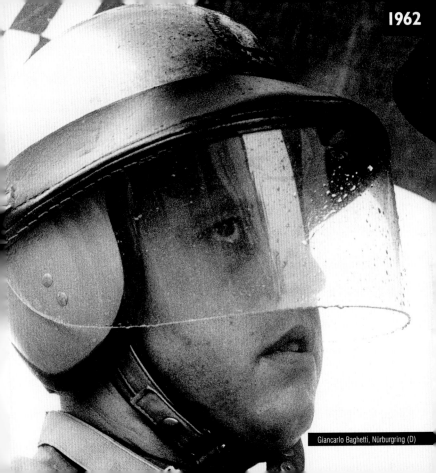

1962

Giancarlo Baghetti, Nürburgring (D)

Ludovico Scarfiotti, Zandvoort (NL)

1963

Willy Mairesse, Spa-Francorchamps (B)

Lorenzo Bandini, Monaco

John Surtees, Zandvoort (NL)

Mike Parkes, Nürburgring (D)

Chris Amon, Monza (I)

1967

Lorenzo Bandini, Monaco

Chris Amon, Monaco 1967

Clay Regazzoni, Zandvoort (NL)

Ignazio Giunti, Spa-Francorshamps (B)

Clay Regazzoni, Monza (I)

Jacky Ickx, Jarama (E)

Clay Regazzoni, Le Castellet (F)

Jacky Ickx, Le Castellet (F) 1973

VICEROY

BELL

Firestone

Mario Andretti, Jarama (E) 1972

Clay Regazzoni, Zeltweg (A) 1975

Niki Lauda, Nürburgring (D) 1976

1977

Niki Lauda, Hockenheim (D)

Niki Lauda, Hockenheim (D)

Jody Scheckter, Hockenheim (D) 1979

Jody Scheckter, Dijon-Prenois (F) 1979

Didier Pironi, Zeltweg (A)

Didier Pironi, Dijon-Prenois (F)

1981

Gilles Villeneuve, Zeltweg (A)

Patrick Tambay, Dijon-Prenois (CH) 1982

René Arnoux, Monaco

Stefan Johansson, Le Castellet (F) 1986

Michele Alboreto, Imola (RSM) 1984

Gerhard Berger, Jerez (E)

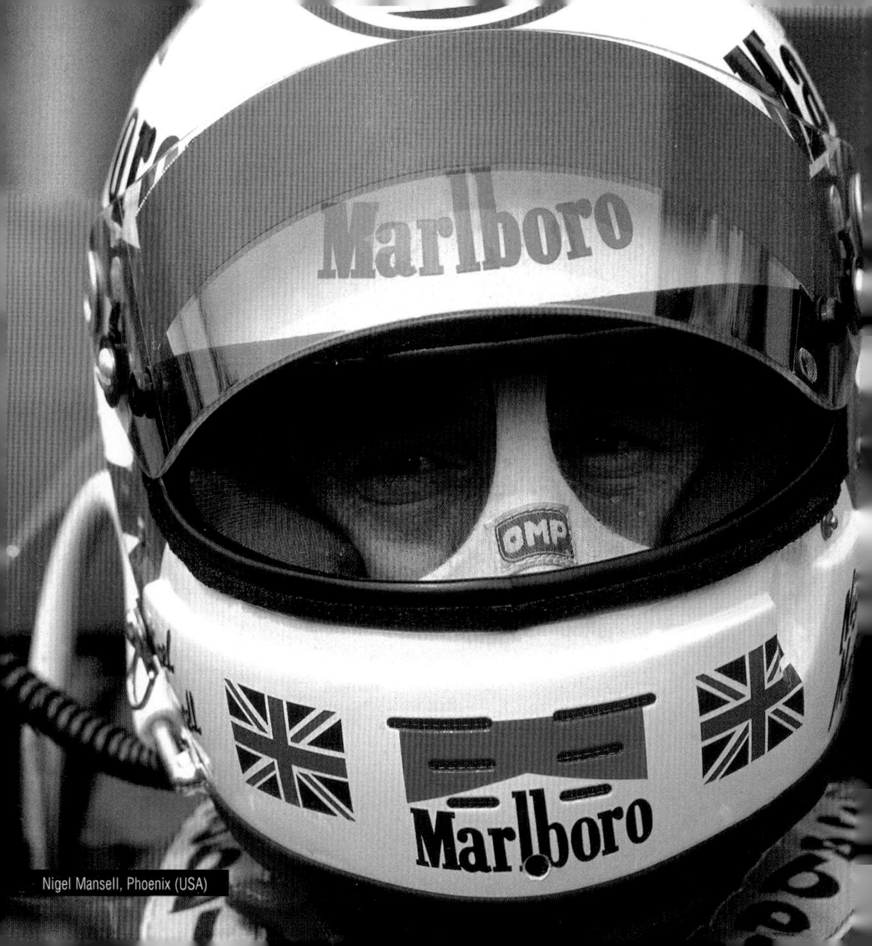

Nigel Mansell, Phoenix (USA)

1991

Alain Prost, Phoenix (USA)

Jean Alesi, Hockenheim (D) 1991

Ivan Capelli, Montreal (CDN) 1992

Gerhard Berger, Imola (RSM) 1993

Jean Alesi, Hungaroring (H) 1993

Gerhard Berger, Spa-Francorchamps (B)

Jean Alesi, Barcelona (E)

Gerhard Berger, Estoril (P)

Michael Schumacher, Nürburgring (EU)

1996

Michael Schumacher, Hungaroring (H)

Eddie Irvine, Imola (RSM)

Michael Schumacher, Melbourne (AUS) 1998

Michael Schumacher, Jerez (EU)

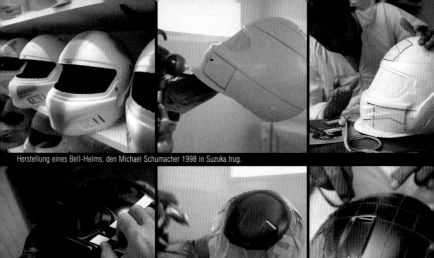

Herstellung eines Bell-Helms, den Michael Schumacher 1998 in Suzuka trug.

Production of the Bell helmet worn by Michael Schumacher at the 1998 Suzuka Grand Prix.

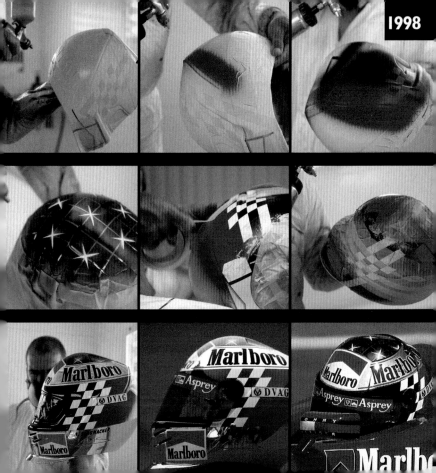

1998

Mika Salo, Hockenheim (D)

Michael Schumacher, Imola (RSM)

Michael Schumacher, Imola (RSM)

Eddie Irvine, Melbourne (AUS)

Eddie Irvine, São Paulo (BR)

Michael Schumacher, Hockenheim (D)

Michael Schumacher, Spa-Francorchamps (B)

Michael Schumacher, Melbourne (AUS)

Michael Schumacher, Silverstone (GB)

Michael Schumacher, São Paulo (BR)

Barrichello (BR)▲   Schumacher (H)▼

Barrichello (RSM) ▲   Schumacher (H)▼

Barrichello (GB)▲ Schumacher (CDN)▼

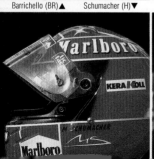

Michael Schumacher, Melbourne (AUS)

Michael Schumacher, Barcelona (E)

Michael Schumacher, A1-Ring (A)

Schumacher (F)▲   Schumacher (I)▼

Schumacher (H)▲   Barrichello (USA)▼

Schumacher (J)▲   Schumacher (J)▼

570

Michael Schumacher, São Paulo (BR)

Michael Schumacher, São Paulo (BR)

Michael Schumacher, Indianapolis (USA)

Michael Schumacher, Indianapolis (USA)

2001

Michael Schumacher, Barcelona (E)

Helmit of Ferrari-Refueler

Michael Schumacher, Melbourne (AL

Barrichello, Schumacher, Silverstone (GB)

Schumacher, Magny-Cours (

Rubens Barrichello, Monaco

Michael Schumacher, Magny-Cours (F)

Michael Schumacher, Magny-Cours (F)

Michael Schumacher, Magny-Cours (F)

Rubens Barrichello, Silverstone (GB), with Schwarzenegger

2003

Michael Schumacher, Monza (I)

Am Anfang steht der Motor, ein Zwölfzylinder. Das ist 1946, ein stolzes, helles Signal in die Trümmerwüste der unmittelbaren Nachkriegszeit. Der "Gesang der zwölf" behage ihm, sagt Enzo Ferrari kühn. Aber er erhebt seine Vorliebe nicht zum Dogma. Im Gegenteil – vor und ab 1961 hinter den Piloten der Roten herrscht im Verlauf eines halben Jahrhunderts Formel-1-Geschichte eine erstaunliche Artenvielfalt: Da tummeln sich Reihen-Vierzylinder, V6 ohne und mit Turboaufladung, V8 und immer wieder V12 (anfänglich mit Kompressor) bis hin zum Extremwinkel von 180 Grad. Dem Trend zur Uniformität des V10 mag man sich erst 1996 anschließen. Die Straßensportwagen der Marke hat er bis auf den heutigen Tag noch nicht erfasst. Bis 1988 gehört das Schalten zum Hand-Werk des Lenkers. Eine Halbautomatik erleichtert ihm das Leben erst vom F1/89 an und bereitet zunächst viel Verdruss. Auf den üblichen Rohrrahmen folgt 1963 in Monza mit dem Tipo 156 Aero ein Halbmonocoque, Aluminiumpaneelen gekrümmt über einer Rohrstruktur. Pate standen das Flugzeug und der Lotus 25 des ruhelosen Innovators Colin Chapman. Da hat man sich eine kurze Bedenkzeit gegönnt wie später in den Achtzigern: Das Chassis des pfeilförmigen 126/C3 von 1983 ist komponiert aus zwei Schalen aus Karbon und Kevlar, aneinander zementiert und verschraubt, leicht und dennoch von trotziger Widerstandskraft. Damit springt Ferrari auf einen Zug in Richtung Zukunft, der zu Beginn des Jahrzehnts von anderen wie etwa dem damaligen McLaren-Bediensteten John Barnard in Bewegung gesetzt worden ist. Im delikaten Umfeld der aktiven Aufhängung bewegt man sich nur mit dem F93A – in einem jener Jahre, die man in der Scuderia am Ende ganz rasch abhakt.

In the beginning there was an engine, a twelve cylinder. It was 1946, and in its own way it epitomised the rebirth of Italy after the war. Enzo Ferrari said that he indulged in "the song of the twelve". But his predilection did not harden into dogma. On the contrary: during the half century of Formula 1 history so far, an astounding variety of species have dwelt in front of and – from 1961 onwards – behind the drivers of the red cars. There have been four cylinder inline power plants as well as V6 units with and without turbo-charging, V8 and, over and over again, V12 engines (originally supercharged) up to the extreme bank angle of 180 degrees. Only in 1996 did the Scuderia join the trend towards the uniform V10 solution. The marque's road cars have withstood it up to the present day. Until 1988 the gear-change was manual. From the F1/89 onwards, a semi-automatic shift mechanism made life easier for the drivers once its teething-troubles had been overcome. The customary tubular steel ladder chassis was followed by a half-monocoque in the Tipo 156 that took its bow at Monza in 1963, aluminium sheets wrapped around a structure of steel tubing. It had been inspired by aviation practices, as well as by the Lotus 25 created by the restless innovator Colin Chapman, and taken some time to materialise. History repeated itself in the eighties. The chassis of the arrow-shaped 1983 model, the 126/C3 ,was composed from two shells made of carbon fibre and Kevlar, bonded and screwed together, immensely strong and light at that. With it, Ferrari jumped on the bandwagon set in motion at the beginning of the decade by others such as John Barnard, who was then a McLaren employee. Only the F93A had active suspension – in one of the years which the Scuderia passes over as quickly as

Producing a Formula 1 Ferrari in the early fifties was still genuine craftsman's work.

La construction d'une Ferrari de Formule 1 au début des années 1950 est encore très artisanale

D50-Chassis, 1957

V12 1497 , 1950

Four Cylinder in-line 1985 , 1952

Ferrari-Lancia D50 V8, Buenos Aires (RA), 1956

1958

V6 2417 cm , 1958

246. Syracus (Sicily), 1958

1958

246/F1 V6, Syracus (Sicily), 1958

158 V8, Spa-Francorchamps (B)

1964

1512 V12, Nürburgring (D) 1965

246 V6, Monaco

312/F1 V12, Monaco

590

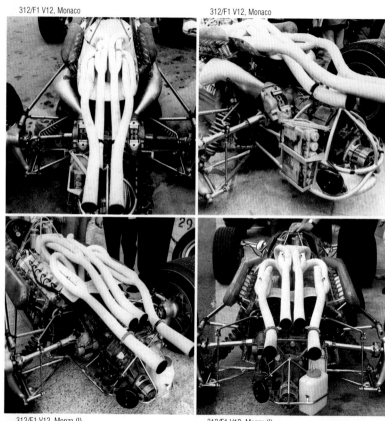

312/F1 V12, Monaco

312/F1 V12, Monaco

312/F1 V12, Monza (I)

312/F1 V12, Monza (I)

312/F1 V12, Monaco

312/F1 V12, Spa-Francorchamps (B)

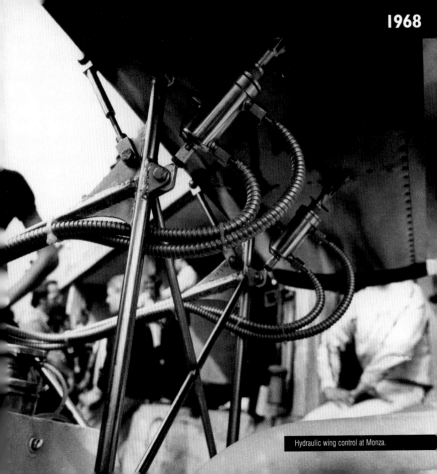

1968

Hydraulic wing control at Monza.

312/F1 V12, Spa-Francorchamps (B)

1969

312/69 V12, Monaco

312/69 V12, Silverstone (GB)

312/69 V12, Silverstone (GB)

312/B, Jarama (E)

1970

312/B, Hockenheim (D)

312/B, Monza (I), paddock-garage

312/B2 Zandvoort (NL)

Britax

312/B, Monza (I) 1970

312/B2, Monaco

312/B2, Clermont-Ferrand (F)

1972

FRAM
FILTERS

MAGNETI
MARELLI

312/B3, Clay Regazzoni, Monza (I)

312/T2, Long Beach (USA)

312/T4, Jarama (E)

1979

312/T4, Jody Scheckter, Dijon-Prenois (F)

312/T4 V12, Gilles Villeneuve, Monza (I)

1979

312/T5, Monaco

312/T5 V12, Zolder (B)

126/CK, Le Castellet (F)

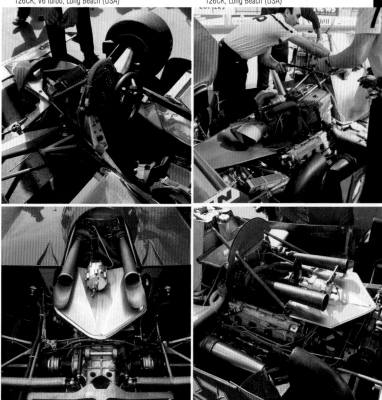

1981

126CK, V6 turbo, Long Beach (USA)

126CK, Long Beach (USA)

126/CK, Long Beach (USA)

126CK, Long Beach (USA)

126/CK, Gilles Villeneuve, Monaco

126/C2B, Monaco 1982

126/C2B, Monaco

126/C2B, Long Beach (USA) 1982

126/C3, Silverstone (GB)

1983

126/C3, Monaco

126/C4, Imola (RSM)

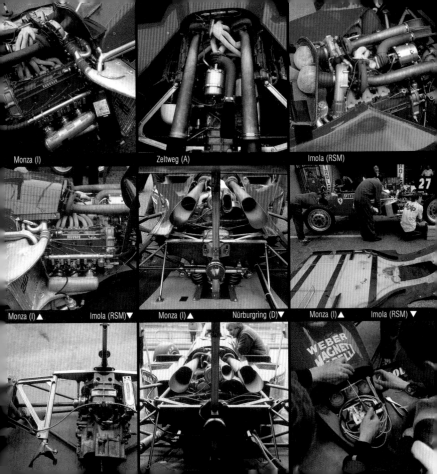

Monza (I)

Zeltweg (A)

Imola (RSM)

Monza (I) ▲   Imola (RSM) ▼

Monza (I) ▲   Nürburgring (D) ▼

Monza (I) ▲   Imola (RSM) ▼

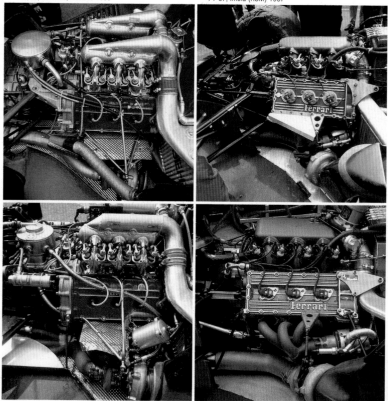

156/85, V6 turbo, Monaco 1985

F1-87, Imola (RSM) 1987

F1-86, Monza (I) 1986

F1-87/88C, Monaco 1988

1986

F1-86, Brands Hatch (GB)

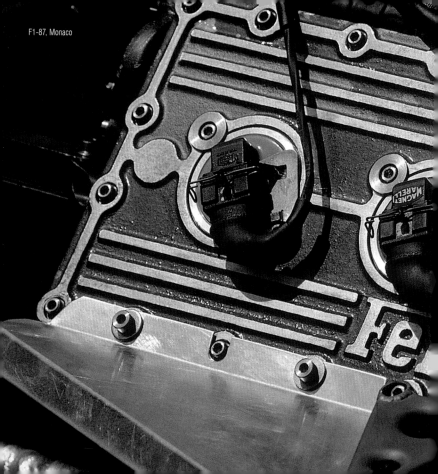

F1-87, Monaco

1987

Brands Hatch (GB) 1986   Zeltweg (A)

Hungaroring (H)

1987

Zeltweg (A)

F1-87, Monaco

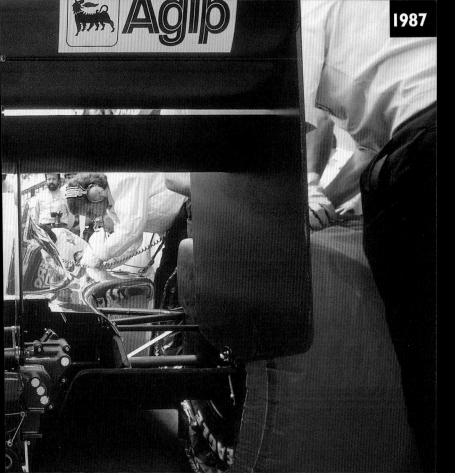

1987

F1-87, Imola (RSM)

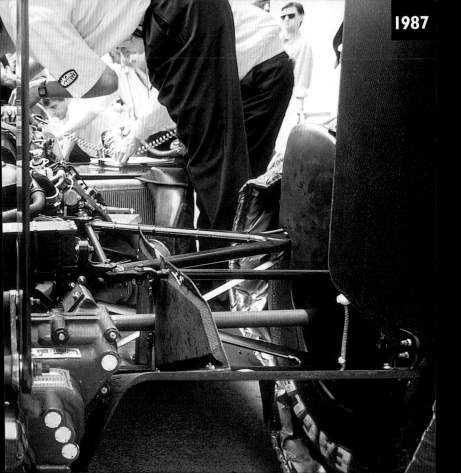

640 V12, Monaco

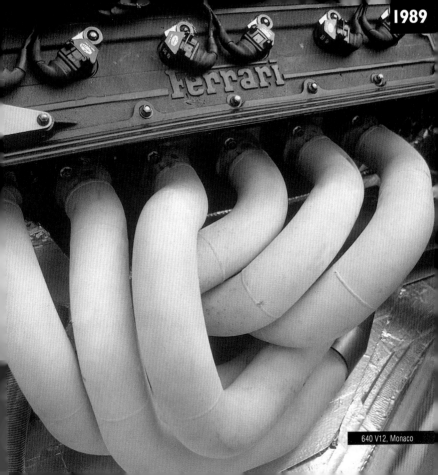

640 V12, Monaco

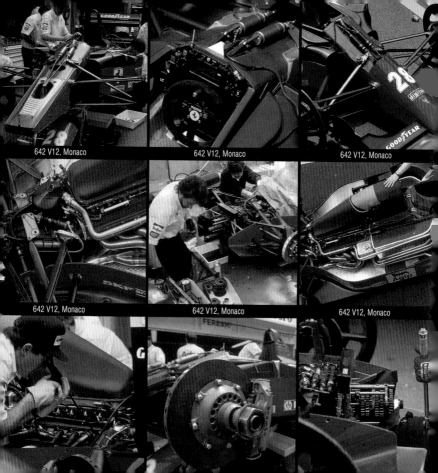

642 V12, Monaco

642 V12, Monaco

642 V12, Monaco

642 V12, Monaco

642 V12, Monaco

642 V12, Monaco

642 V12, Monaco

F92A, Barcelona (E)

Magny-Cours (F)

Magny-Cours (F)

Kyalami (ZA) ▲

Monaco▼

Monaco▲

Monaco▼

1992

F92A, Monaco

Monaco 1993

F93A, Kyalami (ZA)

F93A, active suspension, Monaco

F93A V12, Monaco

F93A, active suspention, Monaco

412 T1, Aida (J)

412T1, Monaco

Refuelling Equipment, Aida (J)

Estoril (P)

Starters, São Paulo (BR)

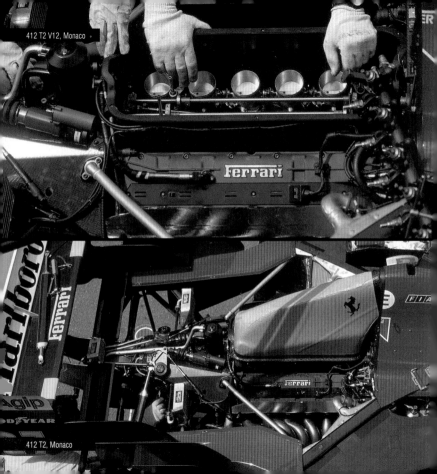

412 T2 V12, Monaco

Ferrari

412 T2, Monaco

GOODYEAR

110 - R

F310 V10, Monaco

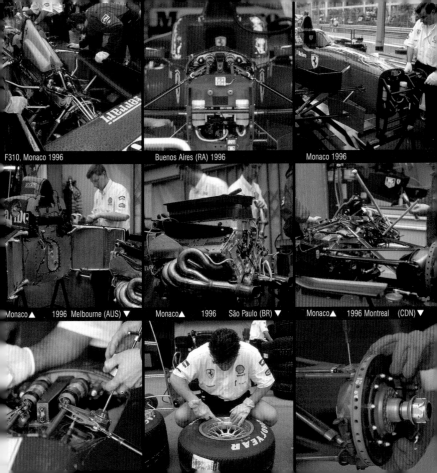

F310, Monaco 1996

Buenos Aires (RA) 1996

Monaco 1996

Monaco▲ 1996 Melbourne (AUS) ▼

Monaco▲ 1996 São Paulo (BR) ▼

Monaco▲ 1996 Montreal (CDN) ▼

Magny-Cours (F)

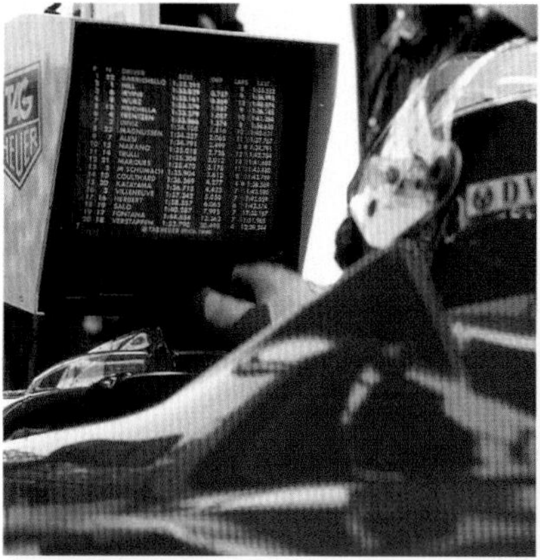

Magny-Cours (F)

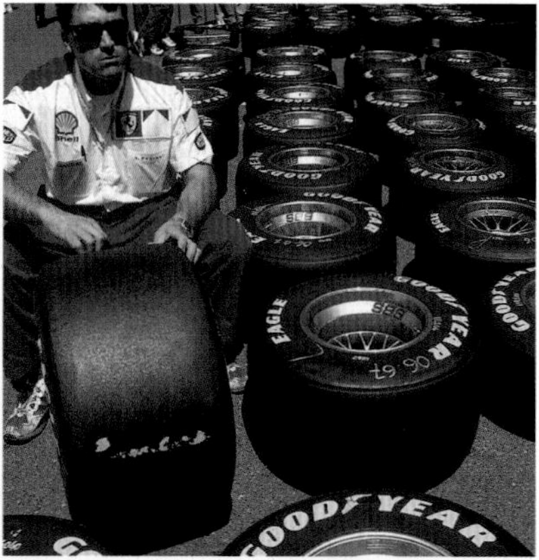

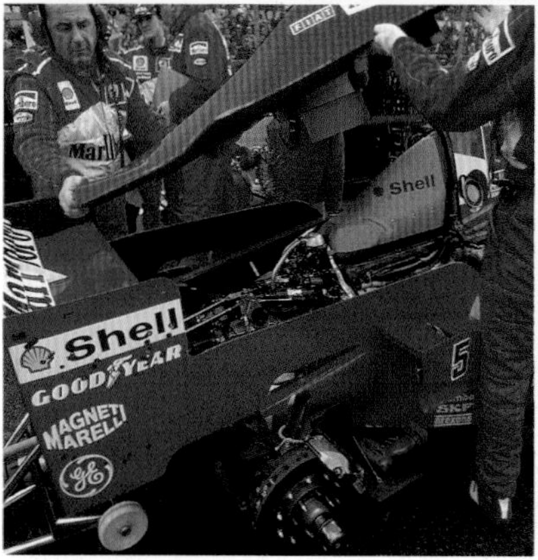

F310B V10, Imola (RSM)

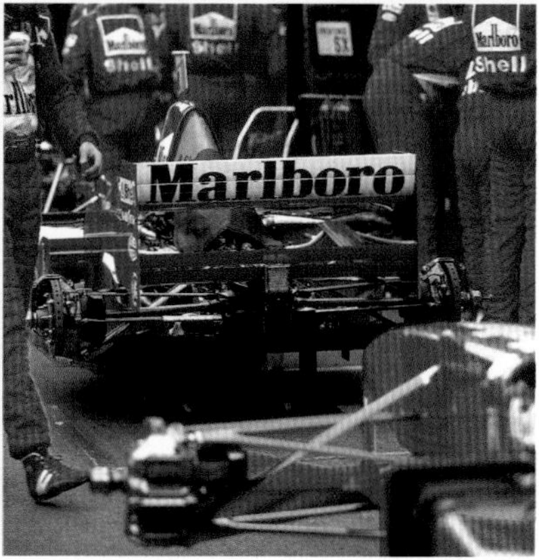

F310B, Monaco

Buenos Aires (RA)

F300, Magny-Cours (F)

Hockenheim (D)

Magny-Cours (F)

Monaco ▲ Magny-Cours (F) ▼

Monaco ▲ Spa-Francorchamps (B) ▼

Silverstone (GB) ▲ Suzuka (J) ▼

Monaco

F399 V10, Barcelona (E)

Monza (I)

Magny-Cours (F)

Sepang (MAL)

Nürburgring (EU)▲   Monza (I)▼

Montreal (CDN) ▲   Monaco▼

Magny-Cours (F)▲   Barcelona (E

1999

Nürburgring (EU)

F1-2000 V10, A1-Ring (A)

F1-2000, Barcelona (E)

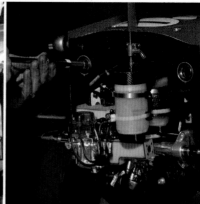

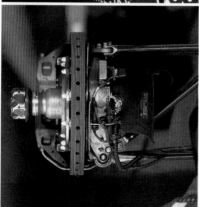

Barcelona (E)

F1-2000, Monaco

A1-Ring (A)

Hungaroring (H)

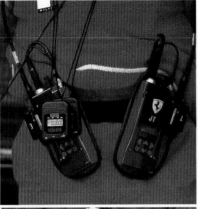

Melbourne (AUS)

Barcelona (E)

F2001 V10, Hockenheim (D)

Melbourne (AUS)·   Barcelona (E)   Magny-Cours (F)

Silverstone (GB)▲   Melbourne (AUS)▼   Hungaroring (H) ▲   Hungaroring (H)▼   Sepang (MAL)▲   Sepang (MAL)▼

Sepang (MAL)

F2002, Monza (I)

F2002, Monza (I)

Drivers seat, Monaco

Montreal (CDN)

F2002, Magny-Cours (F)

F2002, Monza (I)

F2002 V10, Monaco

São Paulo (BR)

Monaco

F2003-GA, Monaco

1951, 375/F1

1952, 500/F2

1958, 246/F1

1975, 312/T ▲

1996, F310 ▼

1984, 126/C4 ▲

1998, F300 ▼

1991, 642 ▲

1999, F399 ▼

1959, 246/F1

1965, 512/F1

1971, 312/B2

1994, 412 T1 ▲

2000, F1-2000 ▼

1995, 412 T2 ▲

2001, F2001 ▼

1995, 412 T2 ▲   F2003-GA, 2003 ▼

Form follows function – bei der Konzeption von Serienfahrzeugen ist das eine Kannvorschrift, im Rennwagenbau ein Imperativ. Ein Formel-1-Monoposto stellt die äußerste Abstraktion des Automobils ohne Schnickschnack und Schnörkel dar. Die zeitliche Umsetzung des Satzes ist allerdings fließend, abhängig vom jeweiligen Stand der Erkenntnis. Auch hier ist Ferrari als einziger Rennstall in der Starterliste von Anfang an mit von der Partie. In den Fünfzigern schickt man im Grunde die Abkömmlinge der Vorkriegs-Dinosaurier an die Front. Es folgt die schlanke und gefällige Glätte der sechziger Jahre. Der Tipo 158, mit dem John Surtees 1964 den Titel gewinnt, ist vielleicht der schönste Ferrari bisher. In Spa sprießt 1968 über dem 312/F1 auf einem Fachwerk von feinen Röhrchen der erste Heckflügel, vorn austariert durch zwei seitliche Spoiler neben dem Kühlermund. Von da werden die roten Renner wie alle anderen zu Zeugnissen der angewandten Wissenschaft vom Wind und von der Wärme: Was muss geschehen, damit das Auto am Boden und auf der Straße bleibt? Wie bewirkt man, dass die Betriebstemperaturen lebenswichtiger Teile dennoch im grünen Bereich bleiben? Das führt zunächst zu stilistischer Unruhe und tastendem Experimentieren, nie ausgeprägter als in der Phase des Umbruchs zwischen dem 312/B2 von 1971 und dem 312/T von 1975. Dabei sind die erfolgreichen T-Modelle der Siebziger gänzlich ungeeignet zum Wing Car – ihre breit bauenden Boxermotoren sperren sich buchstäblich dagegen. Immer mehr wird im Folgenden das Design diktiert vom Computer und dem Windkanal, mit dem F2002 als vorläufigem Höhepunkt: bizarr, zerklüftet – und fast perfekt und unbesiegbar.

Form follows function. That time-honoured maxim may be obeyed when it comes to conceiving a production vehicle. In race car building it's a must. After all, a Formula 1 single-seater is the utter abstraction of the automobile, without any frills and padding. The way the dictum is translated into a respective period, however, depends on the latest technological creeds and crazes. In this respect, too, Ferrari has been part of the grid from the very beginning. The models dispatched to circuits in the fifties were basically offspring of the pre-war dinosaurs. Shapes of slender and attractive sleekness followed in the sixties. John Surtees' championship-winning 1964 Tipo 158 was arguably the most beautiful Ferrari ever. In Spa the 1968 312/F1 model sprouted the first rear wing, supported by a scaffolding of delicate tubes and counter-balanced by spoilers on either side of the radiator mouth. From then onwards, the red cars have borne testimony to the latest insights regarding wind and warmth like all others. What must happen to keep the car on the ground and to the confines of the track? What can be done so that the operating temperatures of essential parts stay within the green range? At first these questions led to stylistic commotion and tentative steps into no-man's-land. That was never more obvious than in the phase of change between the 312/B2 in 1971 and the 312/T in 1975. Paradoxically, the all-conquering T-models of the seventies failed to agree with the wing car concept because of their wide twelve-cylinder boxer engines. In recent years, race car design has been dictated more and more by the computer and the wind tunnel. That parentage is epitomised by the "Red Goddess" named F2002, bizarre, jagged - and almost perfect and invincible.

375/F1, Maranello (I) 1951

375/F1, Bern (CH) 1951

625/F1, Reims (F) 1954

625/F1, Reims (F) 1954

555/F1 »Super Squalo«, Monza (I) 1955

Ferrari-Lancia D50, Monza (I) 1956

Ferrari-Lancia D50, Spa-Francorchamps (B) 1956

Ferrari 801, Rouen (F) 1957

246/F1 Dino, Monaco 1958

246/F1 Dino

156/F1, Nürburgring (D) 1961

1961

156/F1, Monza (I) 1963

156/F1, Monza (I) 1963

158/F1, Monaco 1965

1965

PROVA
MO-49

158/F1, Mauro Forghieri, John Surtees, Clermont-Ferrand (F) 1965

312/F1, Spa-Francorchamps (B) 1968

312/F1, Chris Amon, Monza (I) 1968

312/F1, Chris Amon, Monaco 1969

312/B, Jacky Ickx, Spa-Francorchamps (B) 1970

312/B2, Mario Andretti, Monza (I) 1972

312/B2, Zandvoort (NL) 1971

312/B3, 1974

312/T, 1975

126/C, 1981

156/85, 1985 ▼

126/C2, 1982▲

F1-87, 1987 ▼

312/T2, 1977

312/T4, 1979

126/C3, 1983 ▲

F1/87-88C, 1988 ▼

126/C4, 1984 ▲

F1-89, 1989▼

643, Silverstone (GB)

642, Monaco

642, Monaco

F92A, Kyalami (SA)

F92A, Magny-Cours (F)

F92A, Kyalami (SA)

F92AT, Spa-Francorchamps (B)

F92A, Monaco

F93A, Monaco

F93A, Monaco

412 T1, Monaco

412 T1, Sao Paulo (BR)

412 T1, Sao Paulo (BR)

412 T1, Hockenheim (D)

412 T1, Sao Paulo (BR)

412 T1, Monaco

412 T2, Imola (RSM)

412 T2, Monza (I)

412 T2, Sao Paulo (BR)

412 T2, Sao Paulo (BR)

412 T2, Sao Paulo (BR)

412 T2, Jean Alesi, Estoril (P)

412 T2, Jean Alesi, Estoril (P)

F310, Estoril (P)

1996

F310, Melbourne (AUS)

F310, Magny-Cours (F)

F310, Montreal (CDN)

F310, Magny-Cours (F)

F310, Estoril (P)

1996

Imola (RSM)

F310B, Spa-Francorchamps (B)

F310B, Spa-Francorchamps (B)

1997

A1-Ring (A)

F310B, Melbourne (AUS)

Silverstone (GB)

Jerez (EU)

F310B, Silverstone (GB)

F310B, Spa-Francorchamps (B)

F310B, A1-Ring (A)

Jerez (EU)

F310B, Jerez (EU)

F300, Michael Schumacher, Imola (RSM)

F300, Melbourne (AUS)

F300,Silverstone (GB)

F300, Magny-Cours (F)

F300, Melbourne (AUS)

F300, Spa-Francorchamps (B)

F399, Melbourne (AUS)

F399, Barcelona (E)

F399, Monaco

F399, Melbourne (AUS)

1999

Ferrari Truck, Magny-Cours (F)

F399, Magny-Cours (F)

1999

F399, Magny-Cours (F)

F1-2000, Spa-Francorchamps (B)

Melbourne (AUS)

Spa-Francorchamps (B)

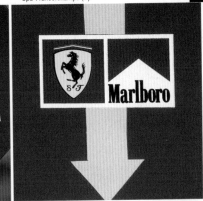

Spa-Francorchamps (B)

Barcelona (E)

F1-2000, Melbourne (AUS)

F1-2000, Hungaroring (H)

Imola (RSM)

Magny-Cours (F)

Sepang (MAL)

Nürburgring (EU) ▲   Sepang (MAL) ▼   Nürburgring (EU) ▲   Sepang (MAL) ▼   Sepang (MAL) ▲   Sepang (MAL)

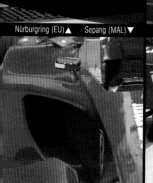

Rubens Barrichello, Imola (RSM)

F2002-Vorstellung, Maranello (I) February 2002

Schwellende Formen unter einem roten Tuch: die rote Göttin.

Pronounced curves beneath a red piece of cloth: the Red Goddess.

Alle Worte, die in betont sachlicher Umgebung gesagt werden, wird die Wirklichkeit in den Schatten stellen.

Whatever words were said in a markedly sober environment were outshone by the reality that was 2002.

F2002, Silverstone (GB)

F2002, Hungaroring (H)

F2002, Hungaroring (H)

F2002, Silverstone (GB)

F2002, Hungaroring (H)

F2002, Silverstone (GB)

F2002, Hungaroring (H)

F2002, Silverstone (GB)

Magny-Cours (F)

Silverstone (GB)

F2003-GA, Monaco

Monaco

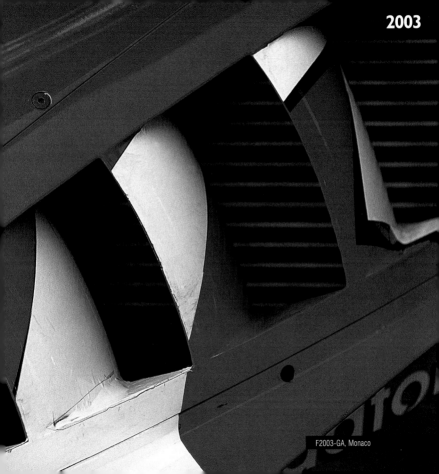

F2003-GA, Monaco

Silverstone (GB)

F2003-GA, Silverstone (GB)

500/F2, 1953

D50, 1956

158/F1, 1964

312/T, 1975 ▲   F1/87-88C, 1988 ▼   312/T3, 1978 ▲   641, 1990 ▼   312/T5, 1980 ▲   412/T2, 1995 ▼

312/B, 1971

312/B2, 1972

312/B3, 1973

126/C4, 1984 ▲   F310, 1996 ▼

156/85, 1985 ▲   F300, 1998 ▼

F1-87, 1987▲   F2003-GA, 2003 ▼

Ferrari – das ist immer auch das Team, die grandiose namenlose Einzelleistung. Ins Schein-
werferlicht der Schlagzeilen oder gar der Buchtitel schaffen es nur wenige. Da ist vor allem
Übervater Enzo selbst, der Alte von Maranello, am 18. Februar 1898 in Modena geboren und
dortselbst am 14. August 1988 verstorben. Er ist ein gusseiserner Autokrat, dessen Wort wie
Gesetz gilt, launisch wie eine Diva, ein weltlicher Papst des Autokults und des Kultautos. Im
Gegensatz zum gegenwärtigen katholischen Oberhirten verlässt er seinen norditalienischen
Vatikan nur selten. Da ist in seiner Nachfolge der charismatische Marquis Luca di Montezemolo.
Zwischen 1973 und 1977 wird der elegante Aristokrat rasch zur rechten Hand des Commendatore
und führt dessen verwaistes Duodez-Fürstentum innerhalb des Fiat-Imperiums seit 1991
immer neuen Höhen zu, wie einst Mitte der Siebziger Triebfeder hinter der roten Dominanz in
der Formel 1. Er kann sich auf vorzügliches Personal stützen: Vor der Majestät des Dreigestirns
Jean Todt als Leiter der Gestione Sportiva, Ross Brawn als technischem Direktor und Strategen
sowie Rory Byrne als begnadetem Konstrukteur von Rennwagen verblassen Ferrari-Größen der
Vergangenheit zu Fußnoten, etwa die Motoreningenieure Gioacchino Colombo und Aurelio
Lampredi in den Vierzigern und Fünfzigern, die Technikchefs Mauro Forghieri und John Barnard
oder die 22 Teamchefs der Scuderia wie Eugenio Dragoni, Franco Lini, Dr. Peter Schetty,
Daniele Audetto und Marco Piccinini. Denn die Sachwalter kommen und gehen, während die
Sache Ferrari Bestand hat – wie die Legende des Commendatore.

Ferrari – that illustrious name will also evoke the team effort, the amazing anonymous individual achievement. Indeed, not many protagonists of the Prancing Horse marque have risen to be in the limelight of headlines or even book-titles. There was, first of all, the man himself, the Maranello enigma, born in Modena on 18 February 1898 and deceased there on 14 August 1988. He was a cast-iron autocrat whose word was law, wilful like a diva, a mundane pope in a realm of automobile worship, the objects of which he had created. Unlike his present ecclesiastical Catholic counterpart, he did not leave his secular North Italian Vatican very often. There is his successor, the charismatic Marquis Luca di Montezemolo. Between 1973 and 1977 the elegant aristocrat quickly became the right hand of the Commendatore, guiding his duodecimo principality within the Fiat empire to ever new heights after 1991. As early as the mid-seventies he had been the moving force behind the red supremacy in Formula 1. He can count on excellent staff: The triumvirate consisting of Jean Todt as the boss of the Gestione Sportiva, Ross Brawn as Technical Director and shrewd strategist and Rory Byrne as an inspired constructor of racing cars, has long outshone Ferrari greats of the past. These include the engine specialists Gioacchino Colombo and Aurelio Lampredi in the forties and fifties, technical wizards like Mauro Forghieri and John Barnard as well as the 22 Scuderia team managers before Todt, such as Eugenio Dragoni, Franco Lini, Dr. Peter Schetty, Daniele Audetto or Marco Piccinini. Ferrari employees come and go, whereas the Ferrari cause persists – like the legend of the Commendatore.

Enzo Ferrari, Modena (I) 1951

Enzo Ferrari, Peter Collins

Zandvoort (NL) 1965, John Surtees

Enzo Ferrari, Monza (I)

Enzo Ferrari, Franco Lini, Monza (I) 1970

Mauro Forghieri, Luca di Montezemolo, Brands Hatch (GB)

Mauro Forghieri, Monza (I) 1979

1982

Mauro Forghieri, Didier Pironi, Zandvoort (NL)

John Barnard, Le Castellet (F)

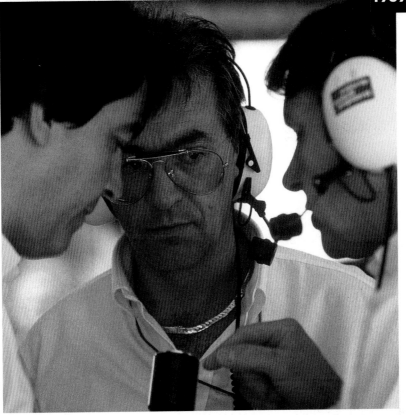

Ralf Hahn, Jerez (E)

760

Piero Ferrari, Monza (I)

Umberto Benassi, Phoenix (USA)

Claudio Lombardi, Hockenheim (D)

Steve Nichols, Imola (RSM)

Phoenix (USA)

Imola (RSM)

Niki Lauda, Estoril (P)

Montreal (CDN)

Barcelona (E)

Hockenheim (D)

Jerez (EU): Jean Todt, Niki Lauda, Dr. Harvey Postlethwaite

1993

Jean Todt, Niki Lauda, Hockenheim (D)

Gustav Brunner, Spa-Francorchamps (B)

Ignazio Lunetta, Imola (RSM)

Luigi Mazzola, Spa-Francorshamps (B)

Osamu Goto, Aida (J) 1994

Monza (I) 1993: Gerhard Berger, Jean Todt

Jean Todt, Jacky Ickx, Monza (I) 1994

Postlethwaite, Ghedini, Lunetta, Spa-Francorshamps (B)

John Barnard, São Paulo (BR)

Dr.Harvey Postlethwaite, Barcelona (E)

Niki Lauda, Donington (EU)

Niki Lauda, Gerhard Berger, Monza (I)

Jerez (EU) 1994: Marco Levrini, Gustav Brunner, Gianni Petterlini, Giuliano Tacconi, Giancarlo Baccini

Jean Todt, John Barnard, Estoril (P)

Beppe Valpreda, Giancarlo Baccini, Claudio Bisi, Nürburgring (EU)

Jean Alesi, Luca di Montezemolo, Buenos Aires (RA)

Osamu Goto, Nürburgring (EU)

Luca di Montezemolo, Buenos Aires (RA)

Giorgio Ascanelli, Imola (RSM)

John Barnard, Estoril (P)

Niki Lauda, Magny-Cours (F)

Jean Todt, Barcelona (E)

Gustav Brunner, Spa-Francorchamps (B)

Claudio Berro, Magny-Cours (F)

Luca di Montezemolo, Giovanni Agnelli, Silverstone (GB)

1996

Jean Todt, São Paulo (BR)

Niki Lauda, Nürburgring (EU)

Nigel Stepney, Imola (RSM)

Montreal (CDN) ▲   John Barnard ▼   Willi Weber ▲   Giorgio Ascanelli ▼   L. di Montezemolo ▲   G. Brunner ▼

Buenos Aires (RA)

Ross Brawn, Jerez (EU)

1997

Jean Todt, Nürburgring (D)

Christian Corradini, Giuliano Zini, Enrico Faccioli, Francesco Uguzzoni, Andrea Genoni, Magny-Cours (F) 1997

1997

Ross Brawn, Jerez (EU)

Hugh Grant, Jean Todt, Liz Hurley, Monaco

Jean Todt, Magny-Cours (F)

Suzuka (J) 1998: Ferrari-Boss Luca di Montezemolo – ein Mann mit vielen Gesichtern.

Suzuka (J) 1998: Ferrari supremo Luca di Montezemolo – a man with many faces.

1999

Luca di Montezemolo, Nürburgring (EU)

Balbir Singh, Magny-Cours (F)

Willi Weber, Nürburgring (EU) 1997

Eddie Irvine, Jean Todt, Monaco

Balbir Singh, Sepang (MAL)

1999

Ivano Romanello, Montreal (CDN)

Fabrizio Grandi, Montreal (CDN)

Stefania Bocchi, Monza (I)

Oreste Giovannini, Monza (I)

J. Todt, L. Baldisseri ▲   J. Sakayama ▼

L. di Montezemolo ▲   Claudio Berro ▼

Ignazio Lunetta ▲   Francesco Barletta ▼

Carlo Cantoni, Magny-Cours

Barcelona (E)

Melbourne (AUS)

Luca Baldisseri, Melbourne (AUS)

Bernie Ecclestone, Jean Todt, Monza (I)

Sir J. Stewart, Carlo Tazzioli, Sepang (MAL)

Ross Brawn, Michael Schumacher, São Paulo (BR)

2000

Jean Todt, Monza (I)

Suzuka (J): Einlösung eines Schwurs: mit Michael Schumachers erster Ferrari-WM fällt Luca Baldisseris Haarpracht.
Suzuka (J): Redeeming a pledge: with Michael Schumacher's first title Luca Baldisseri lost his beautiful head of hair.

2000

Corinna and Michael Schumacher, Jean Todt, Rubens Barrichello

Sepang (MAL)

Jean Todt, Imola (RSM)

Luca Badoer, test driver

Paolo Martinelli, Monza (I)

Luca Baldisseri, Hungaroring (H)

Claudio Berro ▲   Stefano Domenicali ▼

Silvio Ferri ▲   Sabine Kehm ▼

Carlo Cantoni ▲   Ross Brawn ▼

804

Rory Byrne, Imola (RSM)

Jean Todt, Pietro Timpini, São Paulo (BR)

Miodrag Kotur, Barcelona (E)

Luca di Montezemolo, Imola (RSM)

Ross Brawn, Hungaroring (H)

Paolo Martinelli, Monaco

Sabine Kehm, Spa-Francorchamps (B)

Luca Colajanni, Spa-Francorchamps (B)

Hungaroring (H)

Magny-Cours (F)

Rory Byrne, Imola (RSM)

Stefania Bocchi, Silvia Colombo, Imola (RSM)

Luca Colajanni, Silverstone (GB)

Stefano Domenicalli ▲   Ross Brawn ▼   Ozzy Ossbourne, Jean Todt ▲   Chris Dyre ▼   L. di Montezemolo ▲   A. Caselli, J. Todt

Jean Todt, Sepang (MAL)

Melbourne (AUS)

2003

elbourne (AUS)

Marlboro

verstone (GB)

Die drei erfolgreichsten Teams seit 1975
The three most successful teams since 1975

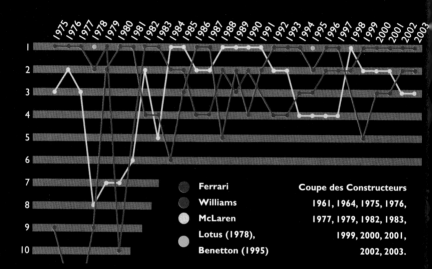

Ferrari
Williams
McLaren
Lotus (1978),
Benetton (1995)

Coupe des Constructeurs
1961, 1964, 1975, 1976,
1977, 1979, 1982, 1983,
1999, 2000, 2001,
2002, 2003.

Abgesehen von den beiden Stippvisiten durch Lotus (1978) und Benetton (1995) machten in den letzten drei Dekaden Ferrari, McLaren und Williams die Konstrukteursweltmeisterschaft praktisch unter sich aus, bis die Scuderia 1999 zum Vierfach-Schlag ausholte. Seitdem der Coupe des Constructeurs 1958 zum ersten Mal ausgelobt wurde, holte Ferrari dreizehnmal die Krone, Williams neunmal und McLaren achtmal.

Apart from the two flying visits from Lotus (in 1978) and Benetton (in 1995), Ferrari, McLaren and Williams have practically fought out the Constructors' Championship among themselves in the last three decades, until the Scuderia tightened their grip on the title in 1999. Since the Coupe des Constructeurs was awarded for the first time in 1958, Ferrari have secured the crown thirteen times, Williams nine times and McLaren eight times.

950	Ascari (5), Sommer (13), Serafini (13), Villoresi
951	Ascari (2), Gonzalez (3), Villoresi (5), Taruffi (6)
952	Ascari (1), Farina (2), Taruffi (3), Villoresi (7)
953	Ascari (1), Farina (2), Hawthorn (4), Villoresi (5)
954	Gonzalez (2), Hawthorn (3), Trintignant (4), Farina (8), Manzon (12), Maglioli (19)
955	Trintignant (4), Farina (5), Gonzalez (16), Maglioli (21), Hawthorn
956	Fangio (1), Collins (3), Castellotti (6), Frére (6), Musso (11), de Portago (15), Gendebien (19), Trintignant
1957	Musso (3), Hawthorn (4), Collins (8), Trintignant (12), von Trips (14), de Portago (20), Castellotti, Perdisa
1958	Hawthorn (1), Collins (5), Musso (7), P. Hill (10), von Trips (10), Gendebien
1959	Brooks (2), P. Hill (4), Gurney (7), Gendebien (15), Behra (17), Allison (17)
1960	P. Hill (5), von Trips (6), Ginther (8), Allison (12), Mairesse (15)

Abkürzungen
Abbreviations

A	Österreich, Austria	H	Ungarn, Hungary	RSM	San Marino
AUS	Australien, Australia	I	Italien, Italy	S	Schweden, Sweden
B	Belgien, Belgium	J	Japan	USA	Vereinigte Staaten, United States
BR	Brasilien, Brazil	L	Luxemburg		
CDN	Kanada, Canada	MA	Marokko, Morocco	USAE	Vereinigte Staaten (Ost), United States (East)
CH	Schweiz, Switzerland	MAL	Malaysia		
D	Deutschland, Germany	MC	Monaco	USAW	Vereinigte Staaten (West), United States (West)
E	Spanien, Spain	MEX	Mexiko, Mexico		
EU	Europa, Europe	NL	Holland, Netherlands	ZA	Südafrika, South Africa
F	Frankreich, France	P	Portugal		
GB	England, Great Britain	RA	Argentinien, Argentina		

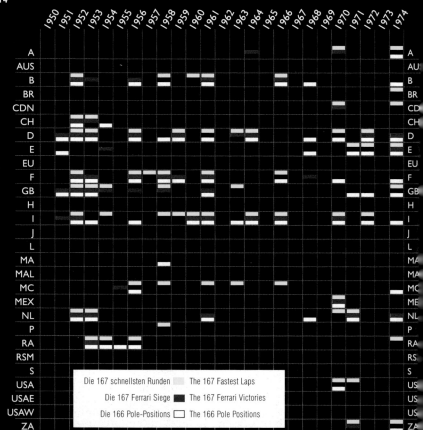

Die 167 schnellsten Runden   The 167 Fastest Laps
Die 167 Ferrari Siege   The 167 Ferrari Victories
Die 166 Pole-Positions   The 166 Pole Positions

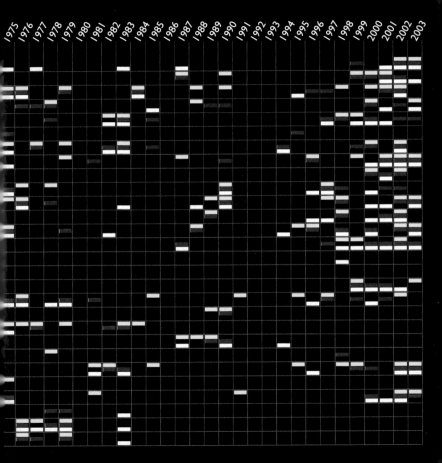

All photographs by Rainer W. Schlegelmilch except:

Collection Maniago: 14/15, 16/17, 18/19, 20/21, 22, 25 bottom, 29 centre, 29 bottom, 32/33, 396/397, 399, 410, 560/561, 562/563, 564/565, 566/567, 654 top, 658/659, 660/661, 664/665, 726 top left, 730

Bernard Cahier: 23, 24, 25 top, 26/27, 28, 29 top, 30/31, 34, 38, 401, 408, 662/663, 666/667, 726 top centre

812: © 2002 grafikartwerk (Stars&Cars 03/2002)

Photography: Rainer W. Schlegelmilch
Text: Hartmut Lehbrink

Graphic Director & Design: Michael von Capitaine
Layout: Rainer W. Schlegelmilch, Stefano Luzzatto
Translations: Hartmut Lehbrink (English)

Production: Michael von Capitaine
Reproductions: Maenken Kommunikation, Köln
Printing and binding: Stampa Nazionale s.r.l., Italy

Idea and Concept: Rainer W. Schlegelmilch, Peter Feierabend

Printed in Italy
ISBN 3-89985-322-9
20-03037-1